40 Fabulous
Math Mysteries
Kids Can't Resist

by
Martin Lee

SCHOLASTIC
PROFESSIONAL BOOKS

New York • Toronto • London • Auckland • Sydney
Mexico City • New Delhi • Hong Kong • Buenos Aires

Dedication

· · · · · · · · · · · · · · · · · · ·

To Clark

Cover design by Josué Castilleja

Cover illustration by Jared Lee

Interior design by Sydney Wright

Interior illustration by Kate Flanagan

ISBN: 0-439-17540-2

Copyright © 2001 by Martin Lee. Published by Scholastic, Inc.

Printed in the U.S.A.

Contents

Introduction

Don't you love the thrill of solving a thorny mystery? Most kids do, too. They enjoy challenges and usually respond to them enthusiastically. They experience a unique feeling of accomplishment upon grasping a complex idea or solving a tricky problem.

Providing your students with motivating mysteries to unravel will do more than give them the opportunity to feel good—it will help them experience the power, utility, and elegance of mathematics. It will give them the chance to apply and adapt a variety of appropriate strategies to solve problems—and that is just what the National Council of Teachers of Mathematics (NCTM) advocates in its *Principles and Standards for School Mathematics*, ©2000.

Solving mysteries is about solving problems. According to the NCTM, problem solving is essential to inquiry and to application, and should be interwoven throughout the math curriculum. Math educators agree that students benefit from frequent experiences in working independently and collaboratively to solve problems. NCTM publications state that if problems are well chosen, they can be particularly valuable in developing or deepening students' understanding of important mathematical ideas.

The best kinds of problems are those that students can access on different levels and that challenge them in a variety of ways. Good problems get kids to think mathematically. They require students to apply number sense and intuitive thinking skills, explore patterns, make and test reasonable estimates, show flexibility in thinking, adjust assumptions, work backwards, use manipulatives, make sketches, or even act out situations. The best problems build on and extend students' mathematical language, skills, and understanding. They help students develop and apply a variety of problem-solving strategies. The problems provide students with the opportunity to assess alternative approaches. They afford students the chance to gauge their own strengths and weaknesses as problem solvers.

As they tackle the mysteries in this book, students will become math detectives. As such, they'll need to bring all their skills to an investigation. First they will need to get their minds around each mystery; they'll need to evaluate what they know and determine what information they need to find out. Then they will have to figure out a way to solve the problem. Next they will use that strategy to find a solution, and then determine whether their solution makes sense. Lastly they'll have to decide what conclusions to draw from their findings, and how best to communicate the information to others. As they work their way through each of these steps, students are learning to be creative and flexible in their approach to new situations. They are becoming confident and independent thinkers.

I hope you'll find that the problems in *Math Mysteries* engage your students and enrich your math curriculum. Happy detecting!

Connections to NCTM Standards 2000

Connections to NCTM Standards 2000 (continued)

Using This Book

✳ This book opens with an introduction to the detective team, followed by 40 math mysteries. Not every mystery is appropriate for every class or for every student. Pick and choose as you see fit. Feel free to adapt or adjust problems to suit the ability levels and interests of your students.

✳ A section of teaching notes follows the mysteries. These notes provide full answers, useful pointers, and math background information, as appropriate. Use this section to learn more about the skills and concepts involved in the solutions to the mysteries. The notes and the NCTM chart (pages 6-7) will help you decide whether a mystery is right for your class.

✳ Good detectives not only need to be good listeners, but also good readers and good summarizers. These mysteries utilize elements of mathematics and language arts, as well as other curriculum connections. When students discuss their approaches and solutions to a mystery, encourage them to tell not only what clue they found, but also where and how they detected it. Invite them to bring their prior knowledge and life experiences into the discussion—as any true detective would.

✳ Your students may not regard solving math mysteries as reading assignments, but they are! Use this opportunity to foster better reading skills. Stress the importance of reading each story thoroughly and carefully; students are not just looking for numbers to pluck out and manipulate. There are clues in the text. Invite students to retell the stories in their own words. They can use context clues to figure out the meanings of unfamiliar terms or expressions. Invite small groups to act out the mysteries for classmates.

✳ Although all the mysteries can be solved using mathematical reasoning, few can be solved quickly or directly by simply using one or more arithmetic operations. Help students appreciate that there's not necessarily one way to solve a given mystery and, in some cases, not even one right answer. Encourage them to be flexible, to try different problem-solving strategies, and to be patient. Guide them to look for the clues that are built in to nearly every mystery.

✳ Use the mysteries as class work or as homework. Assign them, or guide students in selecting mysteries on their own.

✳ Assign one or more mysteries at a time. You may wish to display them on a bulletin board, make copies of them, post them on a class Web site, or read aloud some. You might want to place copies in a grab bag. Students can reach in and tackle whichever mystery they randomly pull out.

✳ Most of the mysteries lend themselves to collaborative work. You can determine the best grouping to suit your teaching style and the learning styles of your students. Encourage them to share solution strategies and mathematical thinking. The writers of the *Principles and Standards for School Mathematics* write, ". . . students should reflect on their problem solving and consider how it might be modified, elaborated, streamlined, or clarified." Guide students to acknowledge and respect others' diverse ideas and presentations.

✳ An Investigator's Log (page 111) follows the Teaching Notes. Copy it for students so they can record information they need and/or gather in the process of untangling a mystery. You may want to revise it to include other questions you feel are important for students to answer or customize it to fit a particular mystery more closely. Students can compile their completed Investigator's Log sheets in an Investigator's Portfolio.

✳ Set up a detective "beat" that your math sleuths can check daily or periodically. Provide different resource materials, such as grid paper, rulers, scales, clocks, maps, calendars, coins, sheets of scrap paper, and clues—written by other students and left there as suggestions for approaches or solution strategies.

✳ Solving these mysteries may get students' creative juices flowing. Encourage them to make up their own math mysteries for classmates to solve, or to write down other math mysteries they already know. Students can post these on the bulletin board, in the detective beat area, or on the class Web site.

✳ Encourage students to record any calculations, sketches, and solution plans in their math logs. Here they can also file any mysteries they have written. Some students' writings and solutions may be appropriate for inclusion in their portfolios.

✳ Take the time to tackle these mysteries yourself. Students will benefit from seeing you in the role of a math detective. You can model how to go about tackling a non-routine problem.

✳ Fill out a Certificate of Recognition (page 112) to acknowledge the efforts of each classroom sleuth.

Meet the Detectives

When you meet Emma and Will, the first thing you notice is how much they look alike. That's to be expected—they're twins. They not only look alike, they often see things in the same way.

"I'm the smarter, better-looking one," says Emma (or Will).

"No, I'm the one with the brains and the good looks," disagrees Will (or Emma).

"No, I am," protests Emma (or Will).

"No way," replies Will (or Emma).

One thing Emma and Will agree on is that they get a jolt from solving mysteries. They've loved being sleuths since they were little kids. I know, because that's when I met them. You see, I was their baby-sitter. My name is Lump. Actually, it's Lawrence, but "Lump" was about all either of them could manage to say at the time. The name stuck. In fact, it now seems that "The Lumpster," "Lumpie," "The Lumpmeister," and "El Lumpo" are all easier to say than "Lawrence." Whatever. I really don't mind.

No matter what they call me, Will and Emma trace their fascination with mysteries to our adventures in baby-sitting. Together we solved all kinds of nifty little puzzlers and head-scratchers. We solved brainteasers, too, while we were at it. We even unraveled a few enigmas and batted about a conundrum or two.

Over time, Emma and Will got pretty good at being detectives. Actually, they've gotten very good. I can say this with pride: Now that they're 13 years old, they're the second and third (or third and second) best detectives in town. They untangle all kinds of knotty dilemmas for all kinds of people. When they get stumped—which doesn't happen but once in a blue moon, mind you—they come to, ahem, me.

Emma and Will have my very private e-mail address and my even more private cell phone number. When they run up against a particularly thorny stumper and are spinning their wheels, they give me a shout. They know that I'm always at hand. No matter how busy I am with my many businesses and other creative successes, I'll toss them the clue they need to get on the right track. They never hesitate to call on me.

"We don't need to call Lump, do we?" Emma (or Will) might say.

"Nah," Will (or Emma) might answer.

40 Fabulous Math Mysteries Scholastic Professional Books

"Yeah, you're right," Emma (or Will) might agree.

"We don't need him," Will (or Emma) might reply.

"Let's call him," Emma (or Will) might suggest.

"OK," Will (or Emma) might nod.

Anyway, my twin protégés have a nice little detective operation going. Business hours start when homework ends. Emma and Will take telephone calls, e-mails, letters, postcards, and visits in the afternoons and evenings, and on weekends and school holidays. They use their secret weapon—me—and a Big Idea. What's the Big Idea? A deep appreciation of the richness of mathematical ideas. By using a host of problem-solving strategies, some critical thinking and imagination, and solid number sense, Emma and Will solve a multitude of everyday problems that might stump lesser thinkers. This book gives you my recollections of some of Emma and Will's favorite cases. Read them carefully, and try your hand at solving them. Maybe you'll even come up with a different solution method than they did. So, wink at yourself in the mirror, nod to yourself confidently, and rub your hands together with anticipation. Clear the room of pesky pets and annoying kid brothers and sisters. Then boot up your brain and dive in.

Happy sleuthing!

The CD Collection Crisis

"This guy is furious, Lump!" Emma said. "He keeps telling us, 'I want my half! I want my half!'"

Then Will chimed in. "The others are furious, too. They're all furious," he said, "and all three of them are right here in our office being furious together. Today is one of those days I wish I'd had more homework. The office would've been closed."

Emma explained that Hoover and his friends, Amy and Amos, had shown up at the office with a doozy of a dilemma. Their mutual friend, Luis Ruiz, was leaving town. He was moving away but leaving a problem behind. The problem was in the form of a gift. Luis told his friends that he was going to give his valuable collection of CDs to them. The collection contained all the CDs made by Out of Sorts—their favorite singing group.

"Do you follow me so far, Lump?" Emma asked.

"Have you ever known me not to? So where's the problem—did Luis hide the CDs somewhere or lock them up and misplace the key?"

"If it were only that simple," Will interjected. "There are 17 CDs in his collection. The difficult part is how he wants his friends to share the collection."

It seems that Luis wanted Hoover to have half of his collection, Amy to have one-third, and Amos was to get one-ninth.

As I digested the data, the dilemma became all too clear. How does one divide 17 CDs as Luis intended?

"You can't break up CDs, can you?" Emma questioned.

I could hear the exasperation in her voice. I could also hear her visitors, loudly and clearly, even though I held the telephone an arm's length from my ear.

"He said half for me, and I intend to get my half! And 8 is not half of 17!"

"Well, 5 isn't a third of it either!"

"There's no way I'm settling for 1 CD as my ninth! I want 2 CDs!"

While Will tried to calm down the three squabblers, Emma drifted away from the group. She spoke softly into her portable phone. "We tried to figure things every which way using our calculators. Then we tried to get these three to cooperate and divide up the goods in some fair way. Nothing doing. We even called Luis, but he was firm about his wishes. We've hit a roadblock on this one, Lump. Any suggestions?"

I began to tap my pencil on the desk, as is my annoying habit when I do big brain work. Before I hit the desk with my second tap, I hit on a suggestion.

"Emma, why don't you put Will on the phone, so he can hear this, too." I waited for Will to join us. The ruckus was still going full steam ahead in the background.

"I'm not taking one CD less than half the collection! Half the collection!"

"I love Out of Sorts! I demand my third! I won't take less than one third!"

"Don't you dare forget about my ninth! It's only a ninth, but it's my ninth and I want it!"

When I had Emma and Will on the phone again, I started in with the wisdom. "You two have got to change your point of view on this. To solve this mystery, you need to look at the situation from a new perspective."

"A new perspective. OK." I could hear Emma rolling her eyes.

"Change our point of view. Well, all right." I could also hear Will bunching his eyebrows together.

I could tell I wasn't getting through. With a big sigh, I asked Emma and Will if they had any Out of Sorts CDs in the office. They did. "Then use your collection," I told them. "Be good and generous hosts to your 'guests.' You can solve this CD-gift dilemma in two shakes."

There was silence on the line. Their brains were spinning to make sense of my hint. Then I faintly sensed one light bulb going on, then another. I think they heard me loud and clear.

"We hear you loud and clear, Lump," Will yelped. "This thing is all but solved."

"Thanks a million," Emma added. "I think we're ready to adjust Luis's collection so that it can be divided as he requested."

Emma and Will may not know what "two shakes" means, but they know about factors and multiples. In five minutes, the three formerly bickering buddies were on their way. All three were a little puzzled, but they were satisfied. As for our two detectives, they didn't take advantage of the opportunity that presented itself—to swap one of their Out of Sorts CDs for one in Luis's collection that they hadn't heard. Out of Sorts wasn't their favorite music group.

> How did Emma and Will use Lump's advice to solve the CD collection crisis?

The Digging Dog Dilemma

After a case as tricky as the CD collection case, Emma and Will were glad to have a case that took them out of the office. When they got a telephone call from a disgruntled homeowner and dog owner, it was just what the veterinarian ordered.

"My name is Ms. Bowser. I live at 14 Pecan Place. My next-door neighbor is driving me nuts," she complained. "He says that Champ is digging up and chewing his precious tulips."

While Will was wondering who Champ might be, Ms. Bowser continued. "I know my Champ. He would never touch that man's tulips or any of his old flowers. Besides, Champ is always tied by a rope to a post in the center of my backyard. It's a long rope. It limits the area in which he can play to 1,000 square feet. But don't feel sorry for Champ. He's got room to romp. And that room doesn't include stupid old tulips."

Will knew he needed more information. "What is the shape of your backyard, Ms. Bowser?" he asked.

"It's flat."

Oh, boy. Will quickly appreciated that he would be better off getting the data he needed in person. He arranged to go to Ms. Bowser's house the next day. He told her he would bring along his sister.

"OK, as long as she doesn't eat tulips."

"No tulips. Just leave things as they are," Will advised. "Keep Champ well fed and out of your neighbor's yard. We'll solve this thing in two shakes."

(Maybe he does know what "two shakes" means after all.)

Will and Emma bicycled to 14 Pecan Place the next day. They took a measuring tape and a calculator with them.

Ms Bowser was agitated when she greeted them at her front door. "That monster did it again! He accused Champ of chomping! He yelled at him, and now my poor baby is sulking. He's just lying out there in the yard with a hang-dog look on his face. I can't even get him to play with his bone."

"We'll look into it, ma'am. Just lead us to the crime scene," said Emma reassuringly.

Ms. Bowser's backyard was square in shape. A large black Labrador retriever was sprawled in the yard, sulking. A long rope was attached to his collar. At the other end, it was clipped to a short post buried in the center of the yard.

Emma and Will looked over at the neighbor's yard. There was nothing but a low hedge separating the two yards. Then Emma spotted the bed of tulips in the neighbor's yard. Then she spotted the neighbor.

"That mangy mutt is ruining my flowers. I'm going to build a wall ten feet high and then dig a wide moat on my side. That's what I'm going to do. And then I'm going to send her the bill!" he exclaimed, pointing at a steaming Ms. Bowser.

"Hold your horses there, partner," Will replied. "Give us a minute to look into this business." He paused to think and then continued, "May I come onto your property for a better look, sir?"

The neighbor nodded reluctantly. Will made his way through a gap in the hedge. He took out his tape measure and measured the distance from the edge of Ms. Bowser's property line to the bed of tulips. It was a distance of 6 feet.

In the meantime, Emma had brought Champ to life with a bunch of Doggie Doughnuts she always kept handy for just such a situation. She had already measured a side of Ms. Bowser's square backyard. It measured 30 feet.

The two sleuths conferred for a moment while the feuding neighbors fumed. Then Will announced their findings to the neighbor. He spoke loudly enough for Ms. Bowser and Champ to hear. "It seems that somebody or something is chewing up your tulips, sir. They are indeed a mess. But Champ here is certainly not your culprit," he said.

How did Emma and Will reach that conclusion?

The Plucked Pay

Emma and Will get their share of e-mails in the course of a day. Their address, MATHA-HA.COM, is known to many. Most of the messages they get are about puzzles in need of solutions. Some of the solutions come to Will and Emma in a jiffy—if they use a little common number sense.

In fact, a puzzling message was awaiting them when they returned from saving Champ's good name.

The message was from someone named Norman. Apparently, he had been robbed. He claimed that somebody had pocketed part of his pay. It seems that when Norm counted his money at home, he was short. He counted it again. Still short. According to Norm, he counted $490 both times. He claimed that he should have gotten $500. Norm surmised that the dastardly deed must have taken place on a busy street as he walked home. That's what he had done—walked straight home from work. Norm blamed the narrow, cramped sidewalks, and one creepy pedestrian in particular.

Norman explained that his weekly salary had been $360, but he had received a 25% raise that week. Because he was an honest and hardworking employee, he had also been given a one-time bonus of four crisp $10 bills. Norm hadn't spent any of his pay before going home. He had no other money on him, except for his lucky penny, which he always carried.

He asked if Will and Emma would meet him at the corner of Market and Main Streets to survey the scene of the crime. He said that he awaited their response.

Norman didn't have to wait long. In a matter of seconds, Emma sent her e-reply. She wrote that although a pedestrian may have given him the willies, that was all this person had done. She explained that there had been no robbery, just a mathematical mistake in a multi-step problem. Then Emma congratulated Norm on his raise and good work, and thanked him for his e-mail.

> **How did Emma know that there had been no robbery?**

A Case of Cast Iron Confusion

Will took an intriguing call one day. It was from a person who had a question about an old building. Helen Armistead Chadsworth was her name, and giving walking tours of the city was her game.

As is customary with people who give walking tours, Helen Armistead Chadsworth had a lot to say and liked to say it. She usually had a lot to say about the city's historical buildings, but one of these cast iron beauties was giving her a pain.

"It's this cast iron beauty I've discovered," she told Will. "It's got me at sixes and sevens."

Now, Will hadn't heard this expression before. "It's got you at what?" he asked.

"I'm confused. I can't place the building. That is, I don't know how old it is. If I don't know how old it is, I'll have a lot less to say about it. And I like to have lots to say about buildings. So do I include this beauty on my tour?"

Now Will was able to guess what "at sixes and sevens" meant. But he didn't know much about Helen Armistead Chadsworth's dilemma. "What—" he began before she interrupted him.

"I spotted the building two days ago during one of my strolls. Although I know that buildings of its type are at least a hundred years old, I do like to be more specific than that on my tours. So I wrote down the address and marched down to the municipal building. Once there, I took the elevator to the fourth floor, walked left, then right, until I came to the Old Buildings' Age Office. I spoke with a clerk there. He was no help. He didn't know why, but for some reason, there was no information at all on that particular old building. I did, however, learn that the clerk was 27, his apartment building was 60 years old, and he had just remodeled his kitchen with marble counters and a double sink. It sounded so very nice. However, I still didn't know any more about my old building—when it was built and who built it. This will not do at all."

Boy, could she talk, Will thought. He asked, "I bet you want me to try to figure out the age of the building."

"Yes, indeed," she replied. "I want you to do it as soon as you possibly can. I've got a tour tomorrow. It's scheduled to begin right after my dentist appointment in the professional offices suites over in the—"

Will stopped Helen Armistead Chadsworth with a short cough. As he had hoped, it prevented her from going on about the precise location of her dentist's office, the wallpaper in the waiting room, the color of the rug, and goodness knows what else.

"Hmmm," he said. "Have you got anything else I can go on?"

Helen Armistead Chadsworth thought for a moment. She couldn't think of one other thing.

"I could go have a look at the building myself," Will said, feeling a little at sixes and sevens himself. "I'm not an architectural historian. I don't know if I'll be able to shed any light on this mystery, but you never know.'

That was okay with Helen Armistead Chadsworth. Will promised that he would go into the city, take a look at the structure, and report back to her.

The building was exactly where Helen Armistead Chadsworth said it would be. Will could see that it was an architectural beauty. So could Emma, who had accompanied him into the city. They looked the building over. They looked at its front, back, and sides. They looked up its walls, right up to the false front of its roof. Then they looked down, to its very base. That's where Emma spotted a design, or what was left of one, in the corner.

The design was made of thin lines that had been carved into the building's limestone base. Some appeared to be curved, while others were straight. Emma and Will bent down to get a closer look.

"What do you make of it, Will?" Emma asked as she photographed the puzzling marks.

"Well, I'll be a gladiator's ghost!" Will exclaimed. He ran his fingers along the lines carved in the limestone, murmuring to himself as he did so. Then he smiled at Emma, clearly impressed with his own cleverness.

"Well?" she asked.

"I know how old this building is, and that it has settled some over the years," he answered.

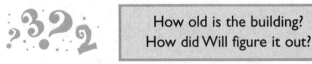

How old is the building?
How did Will figure it out?

The Barbell in the Bag

Every once in a while, Emma and Will's problem solving becomes a family affair. Here's an example of a time when their mom got involved.

Will and Emma's mom likes to go to the gym to ride the stationary bicycle. She generally goes on Tuesdays and Fridays. While she rides, she reads. She catches up on the newspapers that come out on Mondays and Thursdays. Usually, she reads nearly as fast as she pedals. But on Tuesday, October 2, she felt a gentle tap on her shoulder. It was Jim, the gym's manager.

"Have you got a minute?" Jim asked. "I could use your kids' help. I've got a crime that needs solving."

Jim told Emma and Will's mom that three days ago, on September 29, a 150-pound barbell walked off. He explained that the weight would have been far too heavy for only one person to carry very far. He added that a patron of the gym claimed to have seen the two culprits lugging a heavy duffel bag. It seems that Mr. Uphill spotted them carrying the bag between them, Jack-and-Jill style.

"You mean a couple of dumbbells made off with a barbell?" Emma and Will's mom asked.

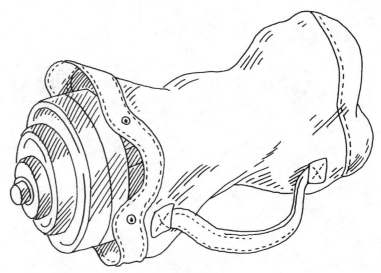

"That's exactly what I mean," Jim answered. "Would you ask Will and Emma to stop by here after school? I would be very grateful."

Jim was waiting for the two detectives when they strolled up to the gym's front desk.

"So, a couple of dumbbells made off with a barbell on Saturday?" Emma inquired. Their mother had filled them in at home.

"Who did Mr. Uphill say he saw?" asked Will.

Jim leaned over the counter and whispered, "He says he saw Belinda R. and Carlos C. carrying the duffel bag together."

"Belinda R. and Carlos C. I know them," said Emma. "Are they regulars here?"

"As regular as Swiss clocks," Jim replied softly. "Belinda, Carlos, and their friend Aaron, too. The three of them joined the gym at the same time in early August. Aaron comes to the gym every other day. Carlos comes every fourth day. Belinda, I believe, works out here every third day. But let me check."

Will and Emma were impressed by how well Jim seemed to know the habits of his customers. Jim turned around the registration forms so that Will and Emma could read them, and pointed to the three names. "Yes, I was right. All three of them first came here together on Thursday, August 2."

Emma and Will looked at the signed forms, each carrying the date of August 2. Then Will reached into his pocket and pulled out his personal organizer. He and Emma looked at the calendar in the organizer. Next they looked at each other and then at Jim.

"The three of them were here together yesterday, weren't they?" Will asked.

Jim nodded slowly. He looked a little puzzled by the remark. "How'd you know?"

"We don't know yet which dumbbells walked off with your barbell, but we know that Carlos and Belinda didn't do it," Emma said with confidence.

How did Emma know that Belinda and Carlos weren't the culprits?

The Valuable Vase

The young man and woman were clearly very upset. They were upset on the phone when they first called. They were no less upset now that they were sitting in Will and Emma's office.

"Would you care for a glass of cold water?" Will asked, hoping it would relax the perturbed pair.

"What we care about is getting our vase back!" answered Tony.

"It was so beautiful. And so valuable, too!" added Tonya, weeping as she spoke and helping herself to one of the twin's tissues.

Tony and Tonya, it seems, were newlyweds. The vase in question was a wedding gift from Tony's great-uncle twice removed. They had brought a photo of the vase, which Tonya plucked from her purse and placed in Emma's hands. The photo was all they had now. The vase had been missing for three days. Tony suspected foul play.

"I suspect foul play," Tony said. "This is a very valuable vase we're talking about. My uncle brought it back from Africa."

This uncle, according to Tonya, was a worldly adventurer. He often returned from his travels to faraway places bearing exotic gifts for his grateful family members. On his last trip, he had been exploring the ruins of the ancient kingdom of Nubia, along the Nile River in southern Egypt. He had obtained a magnificent polished black vase with elaborate geometric designs etched onto its surface.

Will looked at the photo carefully. He gave Emma a puzzled look, which she returned.

Tonya added that Tony's uncle said the vase had been made in the kingdom of Nubia thousands of years ago and that Nubians were known for their beautiful pottery. The uncle also told them that the vase had been made by hand, not on a wheel, it was ancient, and it was priceless. In addition, the worldly traveler pointed out that he had gone to great lengths to get it. He instructed them to be ever so careful when handling it. He told them that they probably should have it insured.

"My uncle told us that it's one of the best examples of pottery from that period," Tony said, as he pointed to the basketry pattern in white glaze and then to the date at the bottom of the vase.

"Look at that date—1852 B.C.," said Tonya. "You see what an old and valuable treasure it is! The date is carved right into it. It's almost 4,000 years old. Oh, I can't believe someone walked off with it. What a shame!"

"And we never did get that insurance," Tony lamented.

Tonya began to sob again, and Tony tried to console his unhappy bride. Emma and Will took this opportunity to look once more at the photo. Then they looked at each other sheepishly with that slap-myself-on-the-forehead look and nodded.

Will spoke gently to the distraught newlyweds. "We have some news."

Tonya and Tony stared at Will. "What is it?" they asked.

Will held the photo before them and pointed to it. "This is a very nice-looking vase. At least I think it is, although I'm not really up on my Nubian pottery. But I can tell you one thing for certain: This vase is a phony."

"A phony?! A phony?!" The newlyweds were totally perplexed.

"Yes, a genuine fake, a sham," added Will.

"I know you're both confused and upset," Emma said. "But whoever stole the vase from you will be in for a surprise if he or she tries to sell it."

> **How could Will and Emma tell that the vase was a fake?**

40 Fabulous Math Mysteries Scholastic Professional Books

A Case of Too Much Information

Sometimes, the way a client gives information to a detective can have a bearing on the case. Will and Emma and I have discussed this issue more than once. Chattering clients can clutter a case by giving more information than we need.

"The unnecessary information just gets in the way, Lump," Emma said.

"Sometimes they're so eager for us to get to the bottom of a puzzle, they don't want to leave out anything," added Will.

I'll briefly describe one of these cases. I'll give only the facts, and no more. The case I refer to involved a problem that needed a solution. The problem made its way to me over the phone. It came at 5 P.M. from Will's friend Eva, who was helping her parents with a home improvement project. Eva's job, it appears, was to saw lumber. She was to cut 3 long boards into 5 pieces each. She knew from experience that she could make a cut in 1½ minutes. She said that each board was 6 ft. 9 in. long and 4 in. thick. She would start sawing at 5:30 P.M.

Then Eva asked her question: "My mom wants to know when I'll be done. She asked me 5 minutes ago. I'm all confused. What should I tell her?"

I told her how long it would take her to cut all the pieces. I even told her how I figured it out. (And I didn't complain at all about all the unnecessary information she had given me. That's the kind of courteous fellow I am.)

How long will it take Eva to complete the sawing?
What information did she give that Lump did not need?

A Case of Too Little Information

Will, Emma, and I have also talked about the problems that arise when a client leaves out information. That happens a lot, unfortunately. Take, for example, a case Will had recently.

It was 9:30 in the evening, and Will was taking a last look at his e-mail messages. There was one from Ralph, one of his grandfather's oldest and dearest friends. Will was surprised. He hadn't even known that old Ralph had a computer. The message had its share of friendly chatter, but it also contained a problem that had Ralph good and stumped.

Ralph, it seems, was in a charitable mood and wanted to give a gift of money to each of his grandkids. He had decided to split $100 among them. His idea was to give each grandchild $5 more than the next younger grandchild. His question for Will was, "How much do I give to my youngest grandchild?"

It was late, and Will was a little tired. The first thing he thought was, *How can I get my grandfather to think more like Ralph here?* Then, without thinking, Will began to jot down some computations. He figured that he could solve this little puzzle easily by writing and solving an equation. Simple. Will wrote the following: x = the amount of money the youngest lucky grandchild would get. Then he stopped. He put down his No. 2 pencil and sighed. Before he could go any further, he had a question that Ralph had to answer.

?3?2 | **What information did Will need before he could solve the gift-giving problem?** | 8?5

Mixed-Up Identities

Will and Emma were in the office playing a geography game one day when they heard someone at the door. A white business-size envelope slid under the door. By the time Emma picked up the letter and Will opened the door, the messenger was gone. They heard the roar of an engine as a vehicle sped away.

What was going on here?

Emma carefully opened the mysterious, sealed envelope. Inside were a letter and a newspaper clipping. The letter was not addressed to anyone or signed at the bottom. It was folded neatly in thirds. The clipping was from a three-day-old newspaper. Emma read aloud the clipping.

"Yeah, I heard about it on the news," said Will. "That's a lot of jewelry for five masked people."

"Let's see about this letter." Emma pushed aside the atlas they had been using and replaced it with the letter. She opened it up, flattened it on the cleared portion of the desk, and read it aloud.

> NEWYORK - November 6- A case of jewels with a value of more than $15 million was stolen late last night from Gold's Jewelry. Five masked adults were seen leaving the scene in a dark, late-model van. The police are

You don't know me. In fact, you don't want to know me. But I know you're a pair of hot-shot detectives. Read what I've got to say carefully because I'm only saying it once. They cheated me, the rats, and they aren't going to get away with it. Since I'm a crook, I'm not going to make it easy for you.

Here's the skinny: There are four of these thieves, and each is heading for where he—or she—lives. They have the following names: Clark, Milton, Terry, and Sal. Each is driving his—or her—own getaway vehicle. Each set of wheels is different, too. One of these crooks drives a motorcycle, another a convertible, a third drives a truck, and the last drives a sport utility vehicle. Each rat lives in a different state, as you may have guessed. And each lives in a rat hole in the capital of that state. One lives in Austin, one in Augusta, one in Sacramento, and one in Pierre. That's right, Pierre.

Not one of these hoodlums lives in a state that starts with the same letter as the first letter of his or her name. It's the same for their ratmobiles, too. Clark drives a rusty red truck. You'd think he lived in a state that had a coastline, but he doesn't. The wheels are about to fall off of Terry's motorcycle, and I hope they do. Sal's convertible has a big dent in it. None of their vehicles starts with the same letter as the rat's name or the name of the state where the rat lives in his—or her—rat hole.

I'll tell you one more thing, too. Two of these felons have brown eyes, one has green eyes, and one has blue eyes. I'm talking about that evil kind of cheating-your-pal blue eyes, that weaselly kind of leaving-your-buddy-holding-the-bag brown eyes, and those cheating skunk kind of green eyes. And because I'm angry, I'll tell you that Clark doesn't have green or brown eyes, and Terry doesn't have brown eyes. Hah!

That's all you're going to get from me, sleuths. I'll be long gone by the time you finish reading this illuminating letter. When you catch up to those thieving thugs, say a big "Hello" for me.

"Wow!" Will exclaimed.

"Great. A real crime!" Emma responded nervously.

"Too bad the spurned stool pigeon left us with a puzzle instead of a solution," said Will.

"I guess you can't expect much more than that from an admitted robber," Emma replied.

The two agreed to take the letter to the police. Before they did, they studied the clues at hand, to see what they could come up with that might help the police.

"If we just look at this thing logically, we can make sense of it. If we're able to tell the police where each crook lives, what he or she drives, and what color his or her eyes are, we might be able to contribute something that can help them crack the case," Emma said.

"I agree. Let's get organized."

"Open the atlas, Will. Or do you know the state capitals well enough without using it?"

With that prompt, Will and Emma went about the business of detection. Soon, using the clues they had been given and an organized step-by-step plan, they had their answers.

In which state did each crook live? What color were his or her eyes? Which vehicle did he or she drive?

Squabbling Siblings

The phone rang in the sleuths' office. It was 4 P.M. Donald, a wily eight-year old, was on the other end of the line. "I found that dollar! It was in that library book just like I said it was!"

Melanie, his sister, was also on the phone. "You did not find that dollar, Donald! You took it off my dresser! I know you did."

Melanie and Donald went on like this for several minutes. Finally Emma, who was listening, had heard enough. "You two called, I suppose, to ask me to settle this problem with the dollar. If you don't stop hollering at each other and start answering some questions for me, I'm hanging up."

There was silence on the other end of the line. "That's better." Bickering brothers and sisters were hard to tolerate. "Melanie, you say that there was a dollar on your dresser, but that it's no longer there. Is that right?"

"Yes. The lying little pest swiped it."

"Did not!"

"Did, too!"

"Did not!"

Emma was losing her patience. "All right already! Stop it, you two!" When they were quiet, she spoke again to Melanie. "Was the dollar loose on the dresser top?"

"Yes. I put it there myself earlier this afternoon."

"OK, Melanie, is there a window by your dresser?"

"Yes, there's a window."

"OK. Has it been open or closed this afternoon?"

Melanie looked. "It's been open," she answered.

Emma thought for a moment and then said, "Melanie, have you looked under the dresser or behind it?"

"Hold on."

As Emma waited, she enjoyed the silence. Then Melanie picked up the telephone again.

"Uh . . . I found the dollar," Melanie said sheepishly. "It was caught behind a back leg of the dresser. I guess he didn't take it after all."

"I told you! I told you!" Donald was exultant.

Emma addressed him. "Donald, you say you found a dollar in a library book?"

"Yes, I certainly did. I never took anything from the top of her stupid dresser. I found that dollar in a book like I said I did. I found it stuck near the middle of the book. It was a bookmark, I guess. I even remember exactly where it was stuck."

"Where was it, Donald?" Emma asked.

"Right in the middle, between pages 117 and 118—nowhere near her dresser. And I'm not a liar."

"Yes you are!" Melanie shouted.

Emma stopped listening to the bickering, but she didn't stop thinking. When there was a pause, she spoke. "Donald, maybe you found a dollar in that book, maybe you didn't. You certainly did not find it stuck between those two pages."

"I didn't?" He sounded uncertain.

"No, you didn't," Emma said firmly.

> **How did Emma know that Donald didn't find the dollar where he said he found it?**

A Cool Witness

From time to time, Will and Emma go on field trips. I encourage this for it expands their horizons. It sharpens their wits. It shows them how people act and what they are capable—and not capable—of doing.

In particular, I encourage them to visit the courthouse and sit in on trials. This way, I tell them, they get a first-hand look at what our criminal justice system is all about. One day recently, that's just what they did.

The case they watched involved a theft. Someone had driven off with a horse, bridle, saddle, and even its food. Apparently, this was done by hitching a parked horse trailer to a truck and driving off with it.

The horse and trailer were the property of Clevis Buckboard, an officer of the Spur Hill Savings & Loan in the small town of Spur Hill. Buckboard had a reputation as a model citizen and a sympathetic banker. His fairness in lending money had made him many friends among farmers and ranchers. Buckboard was known in those parts as "The Loan Arranger." He had a ranch of his own. His horse and trailer had been stolen from there.

A few days later, the horse and trailer were found on property belonging to Cat Purnell. She pleaded innocent. It was her trial that Emma and Will observed. They watched intently as the prosecution trotted out its witnesses. One after another pointed a finger at Cat. Some claimed they saw her pass them on the road. Others say they spotted her driving the trailer onto her ranch. It wasn't looking good for Cat Purnell. When the prosecution was finished, the defense called its lone witness, Lefty. Lefty worked on and off for some of the local ranches.

The defense attorney questioned Lefty. "You say, sir, that you were on Clevis Buckboard's property on the day the crime was committed?"

"I was there sure as birds fly south in the winter," Lefty responded. "I was working for him then."

"And you claim you saw someone go into Buckboard's barn, hitch up the horse trailer, and drive away with it?"

"I saw all that as sure as I see that big spaghetti stain on your tie," Lefty replied.

The defense attorney looked down at his tie with some embarrassment. He recovered himself and asked, "Where were you when you saw all this?"

"I was working outside, stacking wood. I had just begun to step into the shed next to the barn to warm up a bit. It was freezing cold that day, as cold as the first bite of a frozen fudge bar. Just as I dipped inside the shed, I noticed someone fooling with the barn door," Lefty answered.

"Did you look out to see what that person was up to?" the defense attorney asked.

"Mostly I looked out on account of the long, red, goose down coat the person was wearing," answered the cowboy, "It was an awful lot like the one I know Cat wears. Except Cat's is kind of a green color."

"Then," the defense attorney concluded, "if you know that Cat wears a green coat, and this person had on a red coat, then you know it wasn't Cat who was on Buckboard's property that day heisting his horse."

After the cowboy had nodded in agreement, it was the prosecution's turn to cross-examine Lefty. "Lefty, you say that the person breaking into Buckboard's barn was wearing a long, red, goose down coat?"

"It was as red as a—" Lefty began.

"OK, OK." The prosecuting attorney, who had wolfed down a strawberry shake for lunch, didn't want to hear about it. After quickly looking down at his own tie, he continued with his questions. "We know about the color of the coat. And you did say that it was a freezing cold day. Would you say it was just the kind of day for wearing a long down coat, maybe even a hat and gloves?"

"I know it was. In fact, there's an outdoor thermometer on Buckboard's shed door. I happened to look at it when I went inside. It was 15°C," Lefty recalled.

"The temperature reading affirmed your gut feeling about how cold it was that day. Is that right?" asked the prosecutor.

That was right, according to Lefty—but it also helped Emma and Will affirm something they (and the prosecuting attorney) had been thinking. It helped them make up their minds that the cold cowboy wasn't a reliable witness.

How did Will and Emma know that the cowboy's testimony was unreliable?

An Irritating Inheritance

Nat Kudan never did anything the easy way. He never did things the easy way when he was a boy. He never did things the easy way when he was a young man. Now that he's an old man, he certainly never does things the easy way.

Nat's peculiar ways mean more clients for Emma and Will. You see, Nat has a big family. You can usually find one of them sitting in the detectives' office with some kind of mess to untangle. The other day it was Nat's niece, Libby.

Libby is a nice niece to Nat. No one would say that she wasn't. Her brothers Hector and Dave are nice nephews to the old man, too. Yes, Nat has a nice niece and two nice nephews. He knows this and so, when he made his will, he left a portion of his wealth to the three of them. He told them, too. This would have been well and good were it not for Nat's naughty side.

"You won't believe this will," said Libby. "We hope Uncle Nat lives forever. We love him. But also, if he does, that may give us enough time to untangle this will of his." As she spoke, Libby slid her copy of the will out of a large envelope and placed it before Emma and Will. She pointed out the part about her and her brothers.

The twins read it together. What it said was that Dave, the oldest, was to inherit five times as much money as Libby. Libby, the youngest, was to inherit two-fifths as much as Hector, the one in the middle. The will specified that the sum the three would share was $102,000.

"According to what we read here, you three stand to inherit a big pile of cabbage from Uncle Nat," said Will.

Libby responded, "That may be true, but why can't Uncle Nat do anything the easy way? We can't figure out how much money each of us will get. Help!"

> How much money will Libby, Hector, and Dave get from Uncle Nat?

A Ticklish Tip Problem

The perplexing puzzle that Will and Emma solved for Libby was a piece of cake compared to the brainteaser that awaited them in cyberspace. They received an e-mail from a server at Carla's Café. Her name was Danielle, and she was writing on behalf of herself and two other servers at the café. There was a problem about their tips from the day before. There was a cupboard full of chaos at the café. Emma responded to the message promptly. She invited Danielle to stop by the office and tell them more about the dilemma.

Danielle showed up exactly on time. Will offered her a seat and a choice of tea, soda, juice, or water—with or without bubbles. Danielle sat down, accepted a glass of juice, and began to tell about her tip problem.

The problem, she said, wasn't that people weren't tipping that day. In fact, it was a busy day at the café. The problem was that Danielle couldn't figure out how much money in tips she and her co-workers had earned.

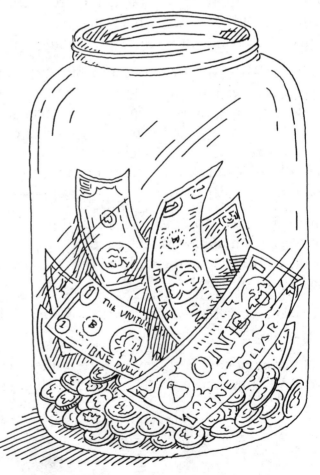

"You see," she explained to the twins, "I work on a shift with two other servers, Ellie and Felix. Every day, throughout the day, we place all our tips in a jar behind the counter. At the end of each day, we divide them evenly."

"You mean each of you gets a third of whatever tips you earned during your shift?" Will asked.

"Yes, that's how it works. That's how it should work. Here's what happened yesterday: I reached into the tip jar just before I went home

40 Fabulous Math Mysteries Scholastic Professional Books

and took my share—one third of the money in it. I left $16 in the jar for the other two servers to share."

"That seems reasonable," said Will.

"If a little low," added Emma.

Danielle had thought the amount was low, too. When she got to work this morning, the $16 was still in the jar! She was flabbergasted. Carla, the café owner, said that both Ellie and Felix had taken their shares of the tips the night before. They had left just minutes before she had the night before. Carla also told Danielle that Ellie took her share first and left, and then Felix took his share and left.

"We each thought that we were the first one to take our third," Danielle said.

Emma frowned. "Now that's confusing."

"Yes, indeed," agreed Danielle. "Now none of us knows how much tip money was in the jar. We don't know how much each us should've received."

Will and Emma looked at one another. Each had been scribbling down figures as Danielle told her story, and each had come to the same conclusion. Will spoke to the baffled server. "One of you knows without knowing that he or she does."

"If you approach this thing from another perspective, say back to front, you'll be able to make some headway," Emma suggested. "Remember, each of you took a third and left two-thirds in the jar."

"Oh," said Danielle, a little wearily. She was thinking that the three servers ought to sit down and divide the tips together from now on.

How much should each server get in tips?
How did you figure it out?

The Bad Art Burglary

There was a robbery right on Market Street in town. All the town's shopkeepers were pretty upset. They had good reason to be. You see, robberies don't happen every day on Market Street.

The store that was robbed was Art's Awful Artwork. Art sold really bad paintings to people with really bad taste in art. Whatever kind of artwork was "out" was "in" in Art's store and displayed prominently. Art was doing a booming bad art business.

Then, early on a Saturday morning before Art opened the store, a thief with particularly horrid taste stole into the shop and made off with one of its most dreadful paintings. The work was so hideous that the few people on the street that morning were too offended to get a good look at the perpetrator. As they turned their heads in disgust, the robber got away unnoticed. Well, almost unnoticed.

Someone did manage to get a pretty good look at the thief. That's the good news. The bad news is who it was—old Nat Kudan. He drives his family nuts with his mischievous ways of doing things. He drives everyone else crazy, too.

At that moment, 8:30 A.M., he was the center of attention. A crowd had gathered in front of Art's store. The police were interviewing witnesses. Nat was infuriating a police office who was questioning him. Emma and Will, who were on a shopping excursion, over-heard the conversation.

"Please, Mr. Kudan, you've got to do better than that. We can't stand here trying to decipher a puzzle. There's a thief putting distance between himself and us with every second of time you waste."

This was not a happy police officer. She tried again. "OK," she said, "I'll try again. Let's start with the time. What time did you spot the thief?"

"I'd rather start with a riddle. Why is a giraffe's neck so long?" Nat asked.

"Mr. Kudan!"

"OK, OK. I'll tell you what. I looked at my watch as the burglar ran from the store. I can say with complete confidence that it was three times as many minutes after 7 o'clock as it was before 8 o'clock. I can say with no confidence what the thief looked like since the painting was between his face and me. Or, was it her face? I can tell you for certain, however, that it was the worst painting I have ever seen."

"Thank you," said Art, who was listening.

The officer was not as grateful as Art. "Mr. Kudan! Is that the only thing you can tell us? You're wasting my time with these riddles."

"Wasting your time? No, I will save you time. For I not only noticed when the thief left the store, I noticed the license plate number of his car. Or her car."

"Why didn't you say so before!?"

"I just did," a puzzled Nat replied.

"Mr. Kudan, please! The license plate number?!"

"Yes, yes, the plate. It had a five-digit number, a palindrome, in fact, with a 6 at each end. Its sum is the greatest prime number less than 30."

The police officer was about to blow her stack. "That's it? That's what you've got for us? Mr. Kudan, there's been a robbery. Some very bad art is in the wrong hands, and you're talking palindromes?"

Nat Kudan thought this over. "You're right," he answered. "I wasn't being fair. None of the digits is a 1, and none are prime numbers. Is that better?"

It was not better. Just as the officer was threatening to haul Nat down to the station to get some straight talk from him, Emma stepped in. She offered to help. "Excuse me, officer, but I think I understand what Mr. Kudan is trying to tell you, in his own annoying way."

Then Emma backed up her claim by unraveling Nat's riddles. She looked down at the notebook she always carried with her. She announced the time of the crime and the license plate number of the getaway car. With this information, the relieved officer called in her report.

(By the way, according to Nat, the reason the giraffe's neck is so long is that its head is so far from its body.)

At what time did Nat see the thief leave the store? What was the license plate number of the thief's getaway car? Explain how you figured out these things.

Mixed-Up Winners

Recently, Will took an award-winning, late-night call. It was from his friend Jack, the student president of the middle school. He was calling about the next day's academic achievement awards ceremony. Jack was in charge of handing out four award certificates to the four students. He sounded frantic on the phone.

"Why do you sound so frantic, Jack? And why are you calling so late?" Will asked.

"You would sound frantic, too, if it was your job to hand out hard-earned awards, and you didn't have a clue about which kid was to get which award," he replied.

"How come you don't have a clue?" Will wanted to know. "Do you know which kids won? Do you know what the awards are?"

"I know the names, and I know what the awards are, but I got things messed up. The certificates used to have the names of the winners clipped to them. They don't anymore. I can't remember which name goes on which award. I should leave town, *now*."

(Although Jack was popular and friendly, he wasn't very organized.)

Will suggested that Jack should call one of the teachers on the awards committee. Jack said he hadn't been able to reach any of them. He also reminded Will that it was almost midnight and a call at that hour would do more harm than good. He appeared to be in a bind.

"I've got to know who the winners are tonight. I have to write a speech about each winner," Jack said. "The awards ceremony is first thing in the morning."

Will thought for a moment. "Jack, you do have a place to start. You know what the four awards are, and you know the names of the winners. What else do you know?"

With some prodding, Jack began to recall more information. The awards were for the subjects of art, science, math, and creative writing. The winning students were Maria, Edgar, Kim, and Tom. Jack told Will something about each student. Maria and Tom were in the eighth grade. Edgar was new to the school this year. Kim seems to win the creative writing award every year.

"That's a start," Will said encouragingly. "Is there anything else you can think of?"

"Yeah," Jack laughed. "I recall that my name, your name, and Emma's name weren't on those slips of paper." Then as he thought for a moment, the day's events began to come back to him little by little.

"You know, Will, I can add a few things to the mix. I remember pieces of a conversation when the teachers came out of the awards meeting and handed me the certificates. A teacher remarked that the science award wasn't going to an eighth grader. Oh, yes. And another teacher said that the math award didn't go to a boy or to a new student."

"What about the creative writing winner?" Will asked.

"I think I heard a teacher say that it was going to the same kid who always wins it."

As Will listened, he had recorded the information in a table. He read the results to his friend. "Jack, I think your troubles are over."

Jack, whose relief could be felt across the phone line, totally agreed. "You're right, Will. I can take it from here. Thanks a million. Now, if they ever give out an award for detecting . . ."

"Good night, Jack."

Which award is each student going to get?

Celebrity (pause) Seating

Emma and Will were very excited. A busy rock music promoter had just called them. The promoter was so busy that he had to interrupt the two-minute call four times to take other calls. Between interruptions, he managed to convey a big problem.

The promoter was hurriedly putting together a benefit concert to raise money for needy children around the world. The performers would be big stars, and the audience would consist of about 700 celebrities. When he explained the problem to the twins, he had their full attention.

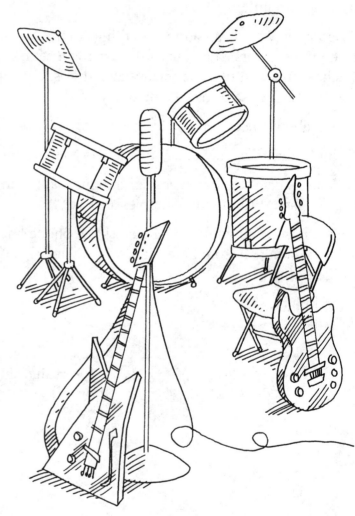

"Here's my problem, and it's a beauty. I'm about to rent a hall for this concert. I'm nervous because I don't know if it will hold all the celebs. Excuse me, I've got to take this call. [pause] OK, I'm back. I've only got a minute or so before I have to make my decision on this deal. If I make a mistake and pick a place that forces me to seat some hot shots on the cold, hard floor instead of on comfortable seats, they'll hit the ceiling. Then my days as an overpaid music promoter putting together shows are over. Excuse me, I've got another call. [pause] I'm back. Where were we? Wait. Hold it. A call. [pause]"

"How many seats does the hall have?" asked Will, as soon as the promoter was back on the line.

"That's my dilemma," the promoter answered. "The owner of the place, Nat something-or-other, tells me that the auditorium has 30 rows. Wait, another call. [pause] Where were we? Oh yeah. He tells me that there are 10 seats in the first row, 11 seats in the second row, 12 in the third, and so on. I'm dumbstruck. Then, to my further amazement, he tells me that I have to figure out the capacity on my own. In fact, he suggests that I look for and use a pattern. Pattern, schmattern, I tell him. How many seats do you have? I ask. To that, the guy informs me that I've got one more minute to figure it out for myself or I lose the hall! I start to mumble, and that's when he tells me that I can make one phone call. He gives me your number. Unbelievable, right?"

Emma replied, "Not for Nat something-or-other. If you'll give us another half-minute or so, I think we can tell you whether or not any celebrities will have to get their behinds cold on the auditorium floor. OK?"

It was OK. In thirty seconds the promoter had his answer. In thirty-two seconds, he was back on the phone closing the deal.

How many people does the hall seat?
How did you figure it out?

In a Pickle

Paula and Paul Pickett have parked themselves in Will and Emma's office. The couple is trying to remember what they're doing there. The Picketts have always been forgetful, even when they were much younger.

"Oh, yes," said Mrs. Pickett. "We're here because we just had our 40th wedding anniversary celebration. We've gotten ourselves in quite a jam. We got some presents, but we can't recall for certain which of our guests gave us which gifts."

"We need to send thank-you notes with the appropriate comments in them to the right people," added Mr. Pickett.

"You remember some things about the gifts and gift-givers, but not everything. Is that right?" Will asked.

"That's it!" answered Mr. Pickett.

"Suppose you tell us everything that you can recall," Emma said.

Mrs. Pickett began to talk. "There were four couples—besides us, that is, at the party. Our cousins, the Ankers, were there. So were our friends, the Wixteds. Our neighbors, the . . . what are their names . . . were there, too."

"The Motts, dear," added Mr. Pickett.

"Yes, the Motts," she repeated. "The Motts as well as our business associates, the Reids, were at the house. Now I can tell you that our cousins live next door to our friends. We saw the Reids about two weeks ago. Was it at a business conference or at the bowling league?"

"It was at the recycling center, I think. Don't forget to tell these two nice young people that we play bridge with the Wixteds every week, dear," Mr. Pickett interjected.

Mrs. Pickett smiled at her husband. "That's right, we do. Thank you, dear."

Will asked, "Was anyone else at your party?"

No one else was at the party.

Then Emma said, "OK. Great. We know who was at your party—the Ankers, the Wixteds, the Motts, and the Reids. Can you tell us what you remember about the gifts you got from these people?"

"I'll try." Mr. Pickett closed his eyes and thought. "We got a lovely toaster—it reminds me of the toaster we had when I was a boy. We also got a large ceramic salad bowl and a, and a, er . . ."

". . . a blender, dear. Remember, we were all shook up when we opened that one. Hee, hee. We also got a lovely pair of candlesticks," Mrs. Pickett said.

Mr. Pickett nodded. "Ah, yes, the candlesticks. Wiggly and very modern looking."

Emma coaxed more information out of the forgetful Picketts. It came out in fits and starts, but out it came. The couple remembered that the Ankers gave them the toaster. They were certain, too, that the Wixteds did not give them an appliance and that their neighbors had not given them either the blender or the wiggly candlesticks. Mr. Pickett added that he was sure that their bowling partners did not give them the salad bowl since that's what they had given the Picketts on their 39th anniversary.

"I can't believe you remembered that, dear," said Mrs. Pickett in awe.

For a moment, all four heads in Will and Emma's office were spinning. The twins excused themselves and huddled over their notes. They began to organize their data to figure out what they knew and didn't know. Soon, they looked down at the table they had created and filled in logically, and then up at the Picketts, who were waiting patiently.

"If you have your thank-you cards picked out, we can help you send the right notes to the right people," Will proudly announced.

"Did we buy the cards already, dear?" Mr. Pickett asked his wife. "I simply can't remember."

"Let's stop by the card store on the way home. One can't have too many thank-you cards, you know," she answered happily.

> Which couple should the Picketts thank for each of the gifts? Explain how Will and Emma may have solved the problem.

A Case from Space

Some problems the sleuths encounter are simply out of this world. Take, for instance, the time they were visited by the Moon family. The Moons had a strange predicament. It was a genuine, intergalactic head-scratcher.

More than two years ago, the family had adopted a boy named Kenneth. He had gotten along famously with all the Moons right from the start—although he was undeniably different in many ways. Both Mr. and Mrs. Moon were in agreement about that. They explained that the differences were due in large part to the fact that Kenneth was from Mercury.

Still, everyone in the household loved Kenneth, and he was treated as a member of the family. For instance, like the other kids in the family, the Moons promised to give Kenneth a car when he reached the age of 20. The Moons hadn't dwelled on that promise very much since their oldest child was only 13 years old at the time. Kenneth had been 12 when they adopted him.

After living with the Moons for a few months, Kenneth went back to Mercury to settle his affairs there. (This is how it works for adopted kids from Mercury and the other planets.) He had to gather all his things and arrange for them to be sent to Earth. He had to get all his papers, including his school diplomas and certificates. Plus, Kenneth wanted to say a final goodbye to all his friends on Mercury. When he had finished everything he set out to do, Kenneth returned to Earth and to the Moon family. He had missed them all very much.

Kenneth had had a lot to do on Mercury, and Mercury is a long way from Earth. He had been gone a full two years when he returned to the Moons' house. Not long after that, Kenneth had dropped a bombshell—and the trouble had started.

According to the Moons, here is what had had happened:

"When do we shop for that car you promised me! I'm so excited! How about a Saturn? No, make that a Mercury," Kenneth said directly and with confidence.

The Moons were stunned. After looking at one another with disbelief, Mr. Moon spoke to the boy. "We're so glad to see you, Kenneth, but what are you talking about? You're 14 years old. You'll get your car when you're 20. You know that."

Kenneth was as startled by their response as they had been with his request. "I've been thinking about my new car the whole trip back here. Does any car manufacturer make a Jupiter or a Neptune? I'd love to drive a Neptune."

The Moons were beginning to lose their patience. "Kenneth," Mr. Moon continued, "you're not getting a car until you turn 20, and that's final. If you keep asking for one right now, I might just change my mind altogether. If I were you, I'd drop the subject."

Kenneth wasn't dropping the subject. In fact, he dropped his second bombshell, and the Moons' jaws dropped when he did it.

"You promised me a car when I reached the age of 20," he reminded them. "You're breaking your promise. You should get me that car. You should get me that car, or I'm going back to Mercury." He spoke firmly, but not angrily since he really didn't want to leave at all. "A promise is a promise where I come from," he added.

Kenneth went to his room to daydream about his new car and to flip through the car magazines he'd picked up at the airport. That's when the stunned Moons had called to make an appointment with Emma and Will.

The twins were as puzzled as their clients were. That's when Will called me. "We're lost in space, Lump, totally flummoxed," Will admitted.

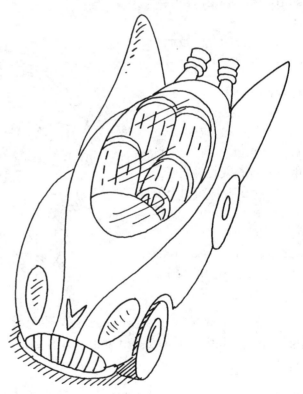

Will then told me everything the Moons had related. I listened carefully. Then I pulled out my almanac and treated the duo to a quick astronomy lesson while the Moons waited. Emma and Will soon "got with the system," so to speak—the solar system, that is.

They reported their findings to the Moons, who were eager for their problem to be solved. "Mr. and Mrs. Moon, you ought to start car shopping," Will said. "By the way, I don't think anyone does make a Jupiter or a Neptune. Do they Emma?"

| Did Will give the right advice to the Moons? Explain. |

Grappling over Grades

"We've got an interesting e-mail message here, Will," Emma said. "Listen."

The message was from Mrs. Lopez and it was about her daughter Lucia. Emma summarized the message for Will. She explained that Mrs. Lopez had just returned from a meeting with Lucia's math teacher. The teacher said that Lucia had an average of about 73 in math. Lucia had told her mother that her average was 91. Lucia, Mrs. Lopez and the teacher both agreed, was not a liar.

"Does Mrs. Lopez give us any more informa- tion, for example, what Lucia's exact test scores were?" Will asked.

The answer to that was an e-mail away. Soon the sleuths had the data. Lucia's grades on seven math tests were 91, 56, 59, 84, 66, 91, and 65. All the tests contained the same number of exercises, and each exam was equally weighted by the teacher.

After a moment with his calculator, Will understood something about Lucia. "It seems that our Lucia is a C student with an A grasp of statistics. Her teacher should be proud, in a funny way."

"So it appears," Emma agreed. "I'll try to clear things up for her mother."

> What should Emma tell Mrs. Lopez about Lucia's math grades? Who's right about Lucia's test average? Explain.

40 Fabulous Math Mysteries Scholastic Professional Books

A Case of Appearances

When K.A.R.P. has something to say, kids always listen. That's because Kids Against Rising Prices is a respected watchdog organization for kids. Its members (all kids themselves) pay attention to what local stores charge for items that kids like to buy. When prices seem too high, the K.A.R.P. watchdogs begin to howl. So, when two young representatives from K.A.R.P. showed up in the sleuths' office, Emma and Will were all ears.

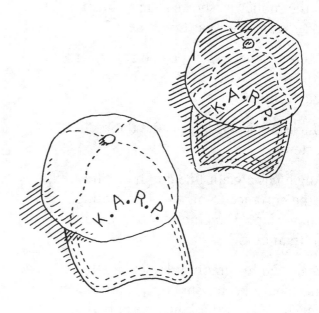

"What's up, guys?" Emma asked. She was addressing two 9-year-old boys, one wearing a yellow baseball cap and the other wearing a green one.

"The CD prices at Uncle Augie's Audio Outlets, for one thing," answered Yellow Cap.

"K.A.R.P. has been keeping track of Uncle Augie's prices for five years. It's been looking at prices of CDs, tapes, and lots of other stuff. CD prices at Uncle Augie's have gone up a dollar a year," Green Cap added.

"That does seem like a lot." Emma agreed. "But there's no mystery about that, is there?"

Yellow Cap rummaged through his backpack. He pulled out a small stapler, tacks, several baseball cards, an electronic game or two, half a baloney sandwich, a sock, and finally, what he was hunting for—a line graph.

"The mystery is the way Augie advertises his prices," Green Cap explained.

"We don't think he's being honest about it," added Yellow Cap, who then showed Emma and Will the graph he had retrieved from his backpack.

"We just learned how to make line graphs in school," Green Cap said, "and we made this one to show how fast CD prices have been going up. Our plan is to post it around the neighborhood."

Will and Emma examined K.A.R.P.'s graph. They agreed that it was correctly constructed and that it accurately showed the data.

Will nodded his approval of the graph. "As far as we can tell, this graph is right on the money. It shows a sharp increase in prices from one year to the next."

"I agree. What exactly is the advertising problem you've come to see us about?" asked Emma.

"Uncle Augie's graph," came the reply in stereo.

"Augie has a giant line graph on an easel at the entrance to his store," continued Yellow Cap. "His graph looks a lot different than ours."

"Yeah. On his graph, it looks like the CD prices have been rising only a little each year. It makes it look like we're barking up the wrong tree, like we've got nothing to complain about," Green Cap said dejectedly.

K.A.R.P.'s Graph

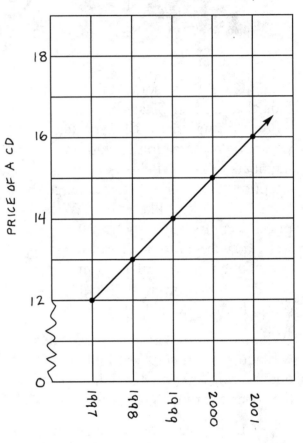

Yellow Cap added that the kids at K.A.R.P. were totally befuddled and that they were confused, as well. He explained that none of the kids could tell which graph correctly showed the information on prices.

Emma and Will looked at each other and then agreed that they had better take a look for themselves at the graph in question. They asked Green Cap and Yellow Cap to come along to Augie's store with them. There, they would settle the matter of the dueling line graphs.

The twins had no trouble spotting the line graph at Uncle Augie's Audio Outlet. It was huge, colorful, at eye-level, and placed smack in front of anyone who walked into the store.

Will and Emma studied Augie's graph to make sure that it showed the same data as the kids' graph did. It did. They also noticed that, according to Uncle Augie's graph, the rise in prices looked gradual. They both sighed before explaining what they noticed to the two anxious K.A.R.P. representatives.

AUGIE's Graph

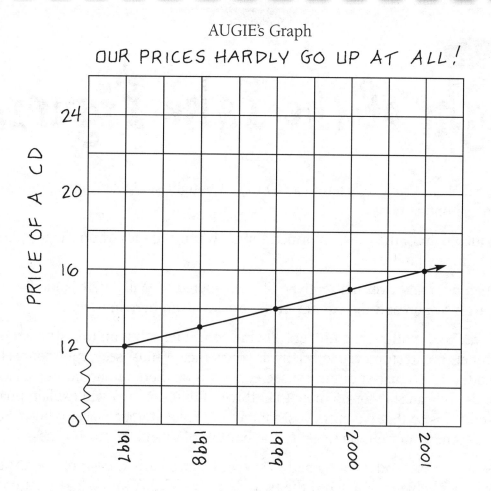

OUR PRICES HARDLY GO UP AT ALL!

"Whose graph is the right one? asked Green Cap and Yellow Cap eagerly.

Emma thought for a moment before she spoke. "I'm afraid that they're both correct, guys. It's just that each graph gives a different visual impression. A look at your graph tells people that there's been a steep increase in CD prices. By contrast, Augie's graph gives the appearance that CD prices have risen very gradually. It's all in the way the graphs have been designed."

Then Will explained to Green Cap and Yellow Cap exactly why each graph looked the way it did. Armed with their new knowledge of the wily ways of the advertising world, the boys thanked the twins for their help and left to share what they learned with the other members of K.A.R.P.

> Why do the two graphs differ in appearance when they show identical data? How does the design of Augie's graph create the appearance of a gradual increase in CD prices? Why does the K.A.R.P. graph give the appearance of a sharper increase?

The Weight of the Fake Figurine

Will and Emma were about to listen to a CD they'd bought at Uncle Augie's Audio Outlet when the phone rang.

"This is Claude Bovine," the caller informed Emma when she picked up the telephone. "I'm calling from my limousine."

Emma clapped her hand over the receiver. She whispered to Will, "It's Claude Bovine, the famous art historian and the curator of the Art Museum here in town."

"I'm on my way to a fund-raising dinner," Bovine continued, "but an unfortunate incident compels me to stop ever so briefly at your office. I must seek your counsel on a delicate matter. It is a matter of utmost secrecy. I will be there in one minute and twelve seconds and can stay for no more than three minutes. Now I will explain precisely what the problem is so that when my assistant and I arrive at your place of business we shall waste no time in our efforts to get to the bottom of this nefarious business."

Mr. Bovine was precise, and what he had to say was particularly intriguing—except for the word *nefarious*, which was a word the twin detectives didn't know. The curator said that there was some bad news, some good news, and then some more bad news.

The bad news was that eight precious and priceless crystal angels had been stolen from the museum's antiquities collection. The good news was that they were returned the next day. The second bit of bad news was that one of the returned angels was a fake; the note of apology that accompanied the returns said so. (Will wondered if all art thieves were as polite as that.)

Bovine, his assistant—and the seven priceless angels and one fake figurine—arrived exactly when he said they would. After exchanging pleasantries with the twins for 22 seconds, Bovine had his assistant carefully remove each of the angels from the box in which it had been meticulously packed. The assistant set them out before Will and Emma.

Then Mr. Bovine asked his question directly: "I have two minutes and thirty seconds to spend here. Then I must dash off. Hurry, hurry, hurry. I must know if you can quickly tell me which one of these small angels is the fake. Not even I, with my trained professional eye, can be certain."

Will looked at the curator, the angels, the curator's assistant, and Emma, in that order. Emma's order of looking was different. She looked at the assistant, the curator, the angels, and Will. Then, at the same time, they each looked at the balance scale they kept handy for occasions just like this one.

"We can weigh the figurines to find out which of them is a fake," Emma suggested with a confident smile. "The one that is lighter than all the others is the phony."

"I haven't time for that. As much as I would love to find out how much a fake master-piece weighs, I'm on my usual tight schedule. There's simply no extra time to be had. I've got less than two minutes now," Bovine replied, after opening his expensive antique gold pocket watch and checking the time.

"We can find the fake with only two weighings," Will assured him.

"Two weighings? A mere two?" the curator asked. He didn't believe it.

"Yes, only two," answered Emma, who pointed out that another few seconds had passed.

"Well, then, I relax in your capable hands," Bovine answered. He watched with great interest and curiosity as Will brought the balance scale to the table and did exactly what he and Emma said they would do. It took two weighings and less than two minutes to find that devilish angel.

How did the twins find the fake with only two weighings? Describe a method they could have used.

Mascot Mischief

It was a bad week for Lincoln High School and its team mascot, which was a log. The wooden wonder had been swiped from its happy home and hustled away by a prankster. Since Will and Emma will attend Lincoln High in the not-too-distant future, the detective duo took an immediate interest in the investigation of this caper.

The twins learned of this case through a phone call. The call didn't come through any of the usual channels—no one in school administration knew about the theft. And that's exactly how Frank Fumble, captain of the football team, and Gary Grumble, equipment manager, wanted it.

Gary explained, "It's the doings of those pranksters at Douglas High. We know it's either Ben, Luke, Theo, Erin, or Marcy. They had the nerve to notify us with a note. Now listen, guys, that's our good-luck log, and we need it back."

"We need it back, big time," added Frank. "Saturday's the big game with Douglas High, and they know where their mascot is."

The Lincoln Logs were in second place, chipping away at Douglas High's lead. Emma and Will agreed to work on the problem, hush-hush. "What about this note? Do we get to see it?" Will asked.

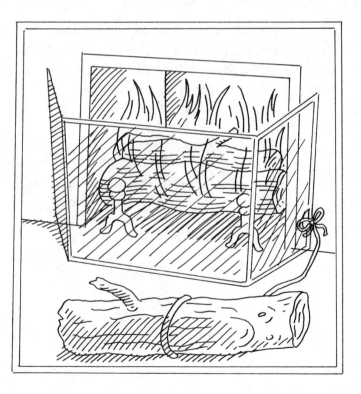

The twins arranged to meet on the sly that night with Frank and Gary. By the swing set in the children's playground, the four of them, using flashlights, pored over the hand-written note together. It was a clever document filled with clues and with wit. But making off with a mascot during football season is no joke. And there wasn't any smiling that night, not even at the attached photo of the poor log being held before a roaring fire! This was sinister business indeed.

After they examined the taunting note, Emma summarized its key points for the group. There were five suspects—Ben, Luke, Theo, Erin, and Marcy. Each one was a teacher's helper, and each had a key to one of the following schoolrooms: language lab, biology lab, geology lab, PE equipment office, and art supplies room, but not in that order. The log was lifted by the person who had the key to the room in which it was kept.

Emma noted that, according to the data before them, the one with the key to the PE equipment office was the boyfriend of the one who helped the Spanish teacher. She said that Marcy was not artistic nor was she taking any language classes this year. She pointed out that Theo didn't have a girlfriend just then and that Luke was a rock hound.

Will spoke next. "I suggest that Emma and I go to our office and organize this data so that we can better evaluate it. If we look at this theft logically, we can settle this reprehensible affair in short order."

"Before you know it, the log will be back in place in the biology lab, and no one in the school will ever know that anything happened," said Emma, confidently.

"And the Logs will be back to their winning ways," Frank chipped in.

After returning to their office, Will and Emma quickly found the solution. They e-mailed the following message to Frank Fumble: Meet us at the office in fifteen minutes. Bring Gary. We're going to pay a surprise visit to a prankster's house to liberate a lost log. Go Logs! Go Lincoln High!

| Who took the lucky log? |
| How did you solve the problem? |

The Sweet Tooth Robberies

I've always had a sweet tooth. Pie is my favorite sweet, and blueberry pie is my favorite pie. I will, however, never pass on apple pie, turn up my nose at a peach pie, or hand back a slice of strawberry rhubarb. Rarely will I refuse a slice of lemon meringue, either. So it was with great sadness that I listened to the tale of woe told to me by Pierre of Pierre's Bakery.

PIES- BAKED FRESH

I am not one to mix business with pie. After hearing his tale, I referred the perturbed Pierre to Emma and Will. I assured him that he would be in good hands with the young sleuths. Then I went to the fridge and fished out a slice of Pierre's deluxe apple cinnamon walnut pie. Yum! Oh, that crust!

Pierre acted faster than I could say, "More pie, please." He called the twins right away. The date was February 1.

"Hello. I am Pierre the baker. I am calling you because Monsieur Lump advised me to. He tells me that he stays away from pie cases, but a pie case is what I have. You see, I am being robbed, and robbed regularly," the baker told Will, who had taken the call.

"Someone has been sneaking into my bakery very early in the morning when I am in the back baking. The thief slips in and then makes off with a pie. The thief takes one pie only each time, and each time a different kind of pie. When I go up front to the counter, I see a space where a warm, fresh, mouthwatering pie had once been sitting. Sometimes, napkins are missing, too. I am at my wit's end."

"I see. This thief can't stay away from your delicious pies. It's an honor, of sorts, I guess. Is there ever any money missing or anything else taken during the thefts?" Will asked.

"No. Just pie. Strawberry rhubarb this last time."

"When was the last time?" asked Emma, who had joined the conversation.

Pierre told the twins that the most recent robbery had just occurred. It had happened bright and early on the previous day, January 31. The theft before that—a cherry pie—had taken place on January 15.

As Will recorded the dates, he asked, "Does anyone work with you in the bakery in the mornings? Are there any delivery people who come and go from your place then?"

"No deliveries in the morning. In the bakery there's only my son Claude, and he is with me all the time. Besides, Claude is not a pie lover or even a cake or cookie fan. Neither is he a thief. My boy could eat anything he wants from the shelves, yet he takes nothing."

"OK, so this is an outside job," Emma said. "You say you've been robbed in the same way, again and again. It could help us to know the dates of the other times you've been robbed. There may be a pattern to these thefts. Do you know the exact dates?"

Pierre took a moment to check his records. Soon, he had some information to relay. He told Emma and Will that pies had been stolen on January 7, and before that on January 3. After a pause, he also added New Year's Day to the list.

"Are there any other days in January?" Will asked.

"No. That's it."

Emma promised to call back Pierre at the bakery within a few minutes. Then she and Will settled down to study the dates. They took out their calendar, too. In the time it might take me to finish off a hefty slab of banana cream pie, Pierre's phone rang.

"It's us, Emma and Will, and we have something for you, Pierre. Although we don't know who's responsible for the pie pilfering, we can tell you exactly when the hungry thief is likely to strike again. With that information, you can be ready to pounce when he or she next appears. Then you can find out why your pies are so irresistible."

Oh, I could tell him that.

> **When will the pie thief strike again?**
> **How do you know?**

Fair Fares?

"That rascal taxi cab driver overcharged me again, Emma! I can explain his cheating in two seconds. Are you listening?"

It was Maureen—again. Maureen was always being overcharged, under appreciated, bypassed, or something of the sort.

"What happened this time, Maureen?" Emma asked politely. She reached for her pad and pencil, settled onto the couch, stretched out, and got totally comfortable. Where Maureen was concerned, nothing ever was explained in two seconds.

I won't bore you with the details of their conversation. It is enough for you to know that half an hour later, when Emma finally and gratefully put down the receiver, she was exhausted. She also had way more information than she needed to respond to Maureen's accusation.

In a nutshell, Maureen told Emma that she'd just taken a five-mile ride in Red's taxi. The fare had been $10.90. A week earlier, she'd taken a two-mile ride in Red's cab. She'd paid $5.65 for that ride. Maureen also told Emma about Red's rates, which were $2.50 for the first one-fifth of a mile and $0.35 for each additional fifth of a mile. She said that these amounts are spelled out for passengers on the side of Red's taxi.

Maureen's accusation went like this:

In the shorter ride, she had traveled two-fifths of the distance she had traveled in the longer ride. Therefore, the shorter ride should have cost two-fifths as much. She said that since two-fifths of $10.90 is $4.36 (which it is), then $4.36 (not the $5.65 which she'd paid) is what she should have been charged for the shorter ride. She understood proportions, she said, and she'd been gypped! Since she'd understood right away that she'd been cheated for the shorter ride, she'd withheld Red's tip for the more recent and longer ride.

(Emma might've told Maureen that, on the other hand, if $5.65 had been the correct fare—based on the prices shown—then it was Red who had been gypped: two- and-one-half times $5.65 is $14.13, not $10.90.)

What Emma did tell Maureen was that Red's fares were right on the money. She went on to say that it was faulty proportional reasoning, not the cabbie's cheating ways that was leading Maureen astray. Emma also told Maureen that she owed Red a tip, and that she could use her proportional reasoning there more successfully.

Where did Maureen go wrong in her understanding of what her fares should have been? Explain how Emma could have figured out that Red charged the correct fares.

A View from Above

Before the letter from Powder Mountain Ski Resort arrived, neither Emma nor Will had any interest in taking up skiing. In fact, neither of them had even heard of Powder Mountain.

The letter was from Debra, the head ski ranger. A photo was also enclosed in the envelope. The letter explained in detail what an airborne ski patrol had spotted from a helicopter while flying above one of the little-used ski runs on the mountain. The photo showed what the patrol saw. What they saw was a set of ski tracks and a tree. But there was something odd about it. The tracks, as you would guess, were two parallel grooves in the snow—until they reached the tree. Then one of the tracks (the right ski, presumably) went around the tree to the right, and the other track (the left ski) went around to the left. Once beyond the tree—below it, that is—the tracks came together again as two parallel lines and continued down the slope.

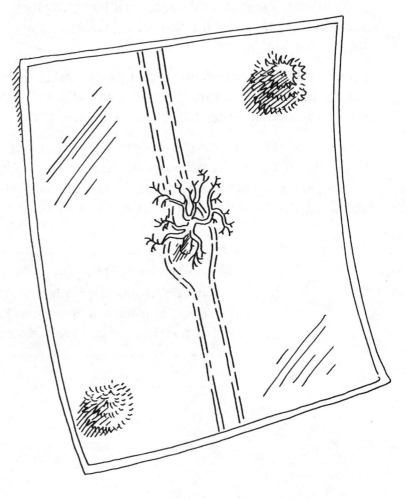

Debra was totally baffled by the photo. She was more than at sixes and sevens. She may even have been at nines and tens! "I simply don't know what to make of this snapshot. What could be going on here? The guys who took the photo are as puzzled as I am. This is all a big mystery to us. We're jumping out of our parkas here; we don't know what we're looking at," she wrote.

In a word, neither Debra nor the others could figure out how a skier could possibly have made those tracks.

40 Fabulous Math Mysteries Scholastic Professional Books

What to one person is an annoying quandary may be an inviting challenge to someone else. To Will and Emma, the ski-track dilemma provided a chance for them put their crack imaginations to good use.

"I have absolutely no idea what in blazes is going on here," Will exclaimed.

"I'm thoroughly in a blizzard," admitted Emma. "Let's dump this one on the Lumpster." (That's when they called me, the last [ski] resort.)

I looked over the photo they scanned and faxed to me. What I told them in my prompt e-mail response was to look at this thing from another perspective. I told them first to think about all the different ways those tracks might have been made. I advised them to then think about that tree, too. I reminded them that the photo was taken from directly above and high above the tree. They appreciated my thoughtful advice, as I knew they would.

"Some help he is," said Will.

"Why do we ask him to help us, anyway?" Emma grumbled.

Still, somewhere down deep in their gray matter, the twins knew that I had given them the tools for getting to the bottom of this snowy impasse. Within a few minutes, they had come up with several imaginative, even plausible, explanations for the appearance of the tracks. They sent their ideas in a letter to Ranger Debra. I know that they were hoping she would appreciate their help as much as they do mine.

> How can the shape of the tracks on the slopes be explained? List as many possibilities as you can. Use your imagination!

Playing a Crook's Game

Detectives have to crack a code or two before they can call themselves real detectives. Will and Emma were no exception to this rule.

A code-cracking case came to them one Saturday via the regular mail. The letter was from a crook—a crafty felon, who generally enjoyed testing the crime-solving skills of the good guys on his trail. First the crook had had his way with the local police, who were utterly baffled by his cleverness. Next he aimed his arsenal of expertise directly at our young detective duo and at their ace in the hole—me. I imagine him smiling as he placed his cryptic message in the envelope.

Soon the smile would fade from his lips. Crooks should be forewarned about me when they think up their codes.

The twins were immediately intrigued by the letter. It had no return address. Their names and address were formed with cut-out letters from several sources, including the local newspaper and restaurant menus. Plus, the envelope was a pale blue, Emma's favorite color.

The letter stated its message plainly and clearly in standard English. The thief claimed to have gotten away with thousands of dollars worth of diamond bracelets, gold necklaces, pearl earrings, and other jewels. He claimed that law enforcement had no leads as to who had taken the goods and no clue as to where the goods were stashed. (All this information, by the way, was provided using letters neatly cut from the jewelry store's own catalogue. Nice touch, eh?)

Believing that he was smarter than everybody else, the confident crook wanted to have fun. His idea of fun was to inform the twins, in code, of the whereabouts of the stolen loot. He boldly challenged them to decipher the code, which would enable them to

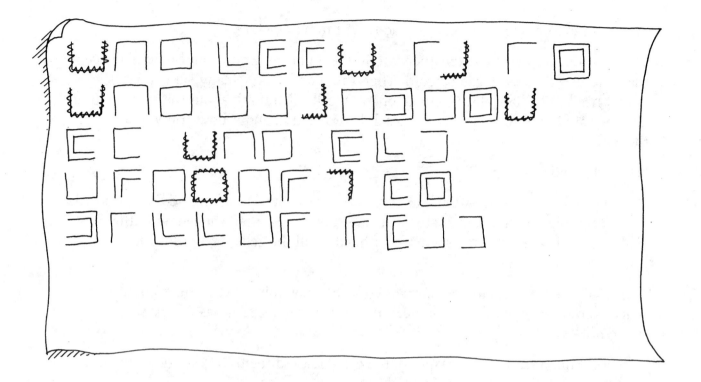

easily recover the take. He wished them luck, claiming that they would need oodles of it. Then he presented his message, as you see it above.

The twins examined the shapes that made up the code. They looked it over from every angle. They looked at it right-side up, side-ways, and upside-down. They held it to the light and looked at it from behind. They smiled and they frowned. They grimaced and they grinned. They knew that with hard thinking they could make short order of the code in no time. They scribbled and they drew. They basked in the challenge. Self-assurance oozed from their pores. The meaning was within their grasp, just about to announce itself to them.

"What in the world is this all about?" asked Emma. "I don't get it."

"I've been clueless in my life," added Will, "but rarely this clueless. I don't understand the first thing about this thing."

In truth, Emma and Will really hadn't yet gotten their minds around the coded message. They needed brain support, the kind they know they can get from me. That's when they gave me a shout. I invited them to fax me a copy of the letter and the coded message.

Now, there are all different kinds of codes. This particular message was constructed using one of my favorites. I worked through it in a jiffy to see that it made sense. It did. Then I returned the twins' call to save the day.

"Do you know how to play tic-tac-toe?" I asked.

"Who doesn't know how to play tic-tac-toe?" Emma replied.

"Think about how many letters there are in the alphabet, Emma, and how many cells there are in a tic-tac-toe game board. Then think about how many game boards you would need to include all the letters, one to a cell. Also think about the most natural and logical flow of the letters within each board. Think about how you would place the letters."

"OK," she said.

"OK," Will said. He was on the line, too, and he was busily making tic-tac-toe boards and filling them with letters in alphabetical order. "I've placed the letters in the most natural way, as if I were writing sentences. I filled in all the cells, except for the last one in the last board," he said.

"Good. That's right," I answered. Then I got to a key point. "Now think about what *shape* each tic-tac-toe cell has—I mean precisely what shape it has. Every shape is different."

Will and Emma studied the shapes of the cells. I asked them to describe some of the shapes to me. They were right on track.

"I'm looking at the message again, Lump. Some cells are made of single lines, some have double lines, and others have squiggly lines," noted Emma.

"Think about this—there are three styles of lines, one style for each of the tic-tac-toe boards."

Silence. Apparently, they needed another clue. Reluctantly, I gave it to them. I told them that the last board was most likely the one with the squiggly lines. (I knew that it was indeed the one with the squiggly lines, but I couldn't give away everything, now could I?)

With that last clue, Emma and Will went to work. They identified the shape of each cell and then found the corresponding letter inside that same shape. It all came together. Soon enough, they had uncovered the hidden location of the stolen jewelry.

The twins shared the information they had uncovered with the police, who were pleased to get it. Will and Emma would've shared it with the crook, too, if they could have.

> **Where did the crook stash the jewelry?**
> **Explain how you cracked the code.**

A Brief Reply

Emma and Will didn't know how to reach the crook from the previous case, but he contacted them again. When he went to the warehouse to admire his haul, he found a surprise instead—no loot! He concluded that his code had been deciphered. He wrote the sleuthing twins another note, which reached them two days later.

This letter, also in code, began with a short note composed of cut-out letters from a police wanted poster. This introductory note said that he looked forward to crossing paths with the young detectives again. The coded message that followed used the type of code that's based on a familiar keypad. This keypad may or may not have a Q or a Z on it. (Now there's a hint-and-a-half for you.) The coded message is shown below.

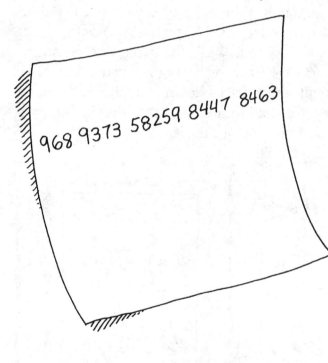

Fortunately, Will and Emma recognized the kind of code the crook had used. Did a call they received earlier that day tip them off? (This is another one of my helpful hints.)

However they managed to catch on, they caught on to the max and were able to decipher the crook's brief message. When they did, they were a little miffed. He was not only a felon, but a sore loser, too! Oh, if they had only known his address. They would've told him a thing or two about being a good sport.

What message did the crook have for Will and Emma? How did you decipher it?

Just Her Luck

Although Kisha is nimble with numbers, she is unlucky. In Kisha's line of work, luck may be more important than brains. Kisha, you see, is a burglar, with a specialty in safe cracking. It is not altogether a bad thing that she has this bad luck.

Kisha can open any lock, unlock any door, or pry open any window. The contents of all safes are unsafe when she's in the vicinity. She's as quiet as a gerbil and as quick as a mongoose but, as I said, she's unlucky.

One time Will and Emma crossed paths with Kisha. As it happened, Kisha's bad luck was at its very best. Read on to find out what happened.

It was a cool and blustery spring Saturday in March. Will and Emma were at the public library. They were doing research for social studies reports. Meanwhile, across the street, Kisha was inside an empty mansion and up to no good. While the twins were having their share of success with the library's resources, Kisha was having her usual dose of bad luck at the mansion. At the exact moment the twins sat down at a table and cracked the books, Kisha was about to crack the safe. She had located it in the study behind a painting on a wall. The twins, of course, knew nothing of this. It was 11:30 A.M.

40 Fabulous Math Mysteries Scholastic Professional Books

Kisha was having a rough time. The combination lock on the safe had 24 numbers, 1-24. The combination that would open that safe consisted of three different numbers chosen in a particular order. That meant, for example, that if 3-8-19 opened the safe, then 3-19-8 or 8-3-19 would not. Kisha knew this and was feverishly trying all possibilities. She knew her own skills, too. It took her only two seconds to try out any three-digit combination. She knew that she could work nonstop until the safe was open. Experience had taught her this and more.

The rough time Kisha was having got rougher by the second. One combination after the next failed. She tried 1-2-3, then 1-2-4, and then 1-2-5. She tried one set of numbers after the next. In the organized manner of an experienced burglar, Kisha tried every possible combination of three different numbers. She did so with all the speed she could muster—two seconds per combination. Still, Kisha had no luck until she had tried the very last possible set of three numbers. The safe opened! Just as she was putting her greedy mitts into the stubborn safe, she heard a noise at the front door.

Like the pro that she was, Kisha didn't panic. Allowing herself a quick "uh-oh," rapidly as a mongoose and quietly as a gerbil, she closed the door of the safe, retrieved her safe-cracking tools from the rug, and clambered through a window in the back—the way she had entered the mansion earlier that day. Fifteen minutes later, she was in a restaurant near her home, eating a bacon cheeseburger. All that time wasted, but she was safe.

Will and Emma had been home for some time already. That night, they watched the 10 P.M. news. Between stories about a big fire and a waterfront festival, they saw Kisha, handcuffed, being taken into the police station sometime earlier that evening. The TV reporter on the scene said that she was suspected of having pulled off a huge bank robbery at the Banco Mundo at 6:00 P.M. He went on to say that Kisha was a crook well known to the police. They had picked her up at a diner, just a block or two from the bank. He went on to report that the suspect was ardently protesting to the arresting offer, Pemberton. She claimed that she was innocent, she had an alibi, and she never even got to finish her burger.

Emma and Will read about the alibi in the paper the following morning. Kisha told the police that she had been too busy breaking and entering somewhere else to rob that bank. The article presented the story she told her captors—that she had been in the mansion's study diligently trying to find the combination that would unlock the safe. She described the safe, its location in the study of the house, and the nature of the combination that opened it. She swore she had had to try every combination before she hit upon the right one. She also swore that she had not taken anything from the safe, despite trying to open it since 11:30 that morning.

(Kisha, you see, would admit to the lesser crime rather than risk being convicted of the greater one.)

"Interesting article. I think she might be telling the truth," Will said to Emma, who had been working something out on her calculator.

"If she is, then she couldn't possibly have been part of that bank robbery. Look." Emma showed the calculator display to her brother.

Will looked at the display, at his watch, and then at his sister. "You're right," he said. "Let's call Officer Pemberton and tell him what we have figured out."

How did Emma and Will know that if Kisha's story was true, she couldn't have commited the bank robbery? Explain your answer.

A Timely Call

Detectives aren't the only do-gooders to get crank phone calls. Crank calls to a pair of teenage sleuths are a nuisance, but they hardly compare, say, with those to a police station or a firehouse. Those kinds of calls are downright evil. Just the same, when a crank caller is wasting a detective's time, someone else might be getting away with a crime. Luckily, the neighborhood was crime-free one evening in late April when Will and Emma's phone rang. The call was from Boston.

"He stole my bike! I saw the thief cut the chain and ride it away. It's a red mountain bike with more gears than an eighteen-wheeler and better tires than a luxury sedan. I want you to get him before he gets too far away!"

Will took the call. He listened politely and then explained that he and Emma didn't "get" anyone, actually. They just figured out who should be gotten. Will also reminded the caller that although he and Emma were in the same time zone as the caller, they weren't in the same city. He added that he could do little more than listen and make a suggestion or two, and that the caller should try the local police.

"I'll take any help you can give. The police won't take the time. Bikes are small potatoes. They hardly ever catch bicycle thieves, not when there are so many more serious crimes afoot. The police are too busy for me and my loss. I know you care, you'll listen. You two bloodhounds will track him down, I know you will. You've got a great reputation. You're the best," the caller gushed.

The best? That was music to Will's ears. He was starting to develop an interest in hearing more about the robbery. Yes, he was a pretty good sleuth. Yes he was, indeed. Emma was too, of course.

"OK," Will answered, "I'm listening. What else can you tell me about the theft?"

The caller revealed that the sun had been in his eyes at the time, but he had gotten a look at the thief speeding away on the bike. He gave Will a physical description of the bike, which was complete in every detail, and of the perp (his word), which, unfortunately, was no better than adequate. The sun was in his eyes, you see.

"The theft of your bike took place just before sunset?" Will inquired. He thought he heard voices and laughter in the background.

"Yeah, I guess," the caller responded. "I didn't notice the time, but the 7:00 P.M. Red Sox game I was watching had just started. It was in the top half of the first inning."

"The first inning in Fenway Park?" Will asked. He had always longed to see a ballgame in the famed old stadium. Fenway Park. The home of Ted Williams. The home of the Green Monster.

"No. Not in Fenway. The Sox are on the road. This game is being played in Anaheim, on the West Coast. Whoa! Another Sox homer! Another homer!"

"That's 7:00 in California?" Will confirmed.

"Of course, California," came the quick answer. "What about my bike? We can't waste time." The caller clearly wanted to miss as little of the game as possible.

Like I said, crank calls are a nuisance. Will was more than a little peeved when he told the creep to buzz off and get a life. Sun in his eyes, indeed.

| How did Will figure out that the call was a prank? |

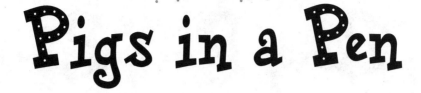

Pigs in a Pen

"Cousin Nat told me that his friend, a pig farmer named Babe something, has 27 pigs. I don't believe it." It was Fran Kudan calling. Her cousin Nat Kudan was a well-known practical joker in town.

"What's not to believe, Fran?" Emma asked. This wasn't the first time that Fran had contacted the twins to ask them to get to the bottom of something that old Nat Kudan had conjured up just to tease his relatives.

"I believe Babe something has 27 pigs," she continued. "How can he have them in four pens?"

"Why not four pens, Fran?" Emma inquired.

"Four pens wouldn't ordinarily cause me to raise an eyebrow, Emma, but Nat also said that there's an odd number of pigs in each one."

An odd number of pigs in each of 4 pens for a total of 27 pigs. Now, that's odd, Emma thought.

"Nat also claims that if Babe took apart his largest pen, he would still have the same number of penned pigs. None would run off or even stroll away. How can that be? I'm off to Babe's farm to find some swine sums. I won't fall for another one of old Nat's goofy games. Care to join me?" Fran asked.

Emma was about to politely decline when the light bulb in her head went on. She told Fran to hang on because a light bulb in her head had gone on and she needed to make a quick drawing.

When Emma returned, she told Fran, "No point in making the trip. Nat's right. I'll draw a diagram and fax it to you."

> How could everything Nat said about Babe's pigs be true? Draw a diagram to prove your point.

Row, Row, Row Your Boat

"Hey, wait until you hear this one, Emma," Will said as he covered the receiver with his free hand. "These folks are in quite a pickle. Get on the line."

Emma picked up the other phone and listened in. She peered over Will's shoulder as he wrote down the information from the caller. The caller, Ed Balin, was speaking on behalf of his entire family—that's Ed, his wife April, and their daughters, May and June. The Balin family was stuck, alone, on an offshore island. They had been on a family camping vacation. Everything had been going along just fine and dandy until a storm came up. The heavy winds had ripped their sailboat from its moorings and sent it, badly damaged, down to Davy Jones's locker. They were stuck on the island—and the island was deserted.

"Whoa!" said Emma, as quietly as you can say "Whoa!"

"You're telling me," Will whispered. "Lucky for them that they have their cell phone with them."

And they used it to call us and not the police or the Coast Guard? Emma wondered.

Emma introduced herself to Ed Balin and immediately suggested the Coast Guard. Ed told her that his family preferred to solve their own troubles. "Luckily, we're not in any immediate danger here," he added.

"How far is it to the mainland? Can you all swim ashore? Do you have any kind of boat at all, or even the means to build one? Could you build a raft?" Emma was full of questions. She has a strong survival instinct.

"It's too far for swimming, especially the way we Balins swim, but we did manage to save our small rowboat," said Ed.

"That's a relief," Will sighed.

"It can only hold 220 pounds without sinking," Ed said.

Only 220 pounds—the Balins surely weighed more than that, Will thought. "How much does each of you weigh?" Will asked.

Ed was ready with his answer. "I'm ready with that answer because all we've been talking about is how to use that rowboat. Let's see. I weigh 180 pounds, and April weighs 135 pounds. May, our oldest, weighs 90 pounds, and June, our youngest, 75. We've got 480 pounds of Balins, but a boat that can carry only 220 pounds of us. We've been thinking of ways to quickly lose lots of weight."

"I'd scratch the weight-loss schemes if I were you, Ed," advised Emma.

"If you give me and my sister a minute or two to think this one through, we might be able to figure out something. You know, where there's a rowboat, there's a way. Let me have your cell phone number. We'll get back to you before you can say 'Robinson Crusoe,'" Will said.

Focusing on what the little boat could handle, Will drew diagrams. Emma used markers. Soon they each arrived at the same plan for the Balins. Will dialed their cell phone number.

"Mr. Balin," he said enthusiastically. "Start gathering your things. We've found a way to get all four of you back to the mainland safe and sound. It will take several trips, though. Can each of you row the boat?"

> How can the Balins use the rowboat to get off the island? Give the step-by-step details of a rescue plan.

Flavors of the Day

The twins don't need to be in their office to do their math detective duties. They might, for example, be at Cones, deeply enjoying one of the 66 delicious two-scoop combo ice cream cones that have made the place a local institution. It was, in fact, on one of those occasions that duty called. It called in the form of Gilbert, who worked at the store. He had a confused look on his face as he approached the twins, who were at that moment occupied with the treats before them. (Emma had a blueberry/apricot cone, and Will had a cup of peanut butter/fudge brownie.)

"Boy, am I glad you two are here!" Gilbert exclaimed. His relief at seeing them was as easy to spot as a big blue ink stain on a crisp white shirt.

"Hey, Gilbert," said Will.

Gilbert wrung his hands. "I'm in a bind."

"What kind of a bind is that, buddy?" asked Will, dripping fudge brownie ice cream on his sleeve. "Yuk," he said as he reached for a napkin.

"The kind in which I'm here alone, in charge, and I can't solve a key problem. That's the kind," answered Gilbert, who didn't drip a thing since he wasn't having ice cream at the moment.

He explained that he had been made manager of Cones for the day while the real manager was away. One of his duties was to smile a lot, which he had been doing until the problem arose. Another duty was to figure out the number of two-scoop cone or cup combination that customers could choose from that day.

"Aren't there 66 different combos every day?" asked Emma.

"Ordinarily that would be true," Gilbert answered, "but the ice cream supplier ran short today. The supplier didn't deliver four vats of ice cream. There's no vanilla banana swirl, no raspberry cream, no chocolate chip muffin sundae, and—worst of all—no peach ginger almond crunch."

"Oh," said Will.

"Double oh," said Emma.

"I have to figure out how many two-scoop cone or cup combos we can offer today," Gilbert explained. "I don't even know where or how to begin."

"Does a combo always mean two different flavors, Gilbert?" Emma asked.

"You wouldn't call two scoops of vanilla a vanilla combo, would you, Emma?' Will interjected.

"Does it matter which flavor is on top—I mean, is a vanilla/chocolate combination the same as a chocolate/vanilla combination?" she asked.

"Yes. A two-scoop combination is two flavors, in any position. Which one goes in the cone first doesn't matter," Gilbert said.

That was all the data the sleuth duo needed to help their friend solve his problem. They pointed Gilbert in the right direction. They suggested that he begin with the number of different flavors it took to make the usual 66 combos. That's just what he did. Within a minute, Gilbert was at the chalkboard, cheerfully recording the correct number of two-scoop combos customers could enjoy that day.

> **How many different two-scoop ice cream combos can Gilbert serve that day? How did you solve the problem?**

Carlotta's Coins

"I won! I won!" Carlotta shouted breathlessly.

"What did you win, Carlotta?" Emma asked.

"I won 10 pounds of something," she huffed and puffed, "just for being the 10,000th customer at Shop & Go Market! It wasn't even my idea. I hate shopping. My mom sent me there for juice and milk."

"You won 10 pounds of something. Well, that's great. I guess congratulations are in order," added Will (who privately wondered what prize would be in store for the one millionth customer).

"If it were just congratulations I wanted Will, I wouldn't have barged into your office to disturb you while you're doing your detecting and all. I came to ask you to help me figure out what I've won," said Carlotta.

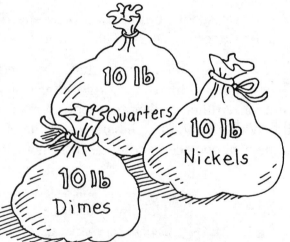

Carlotta had to figure out which of the following was the biggest prize—10 pounds of quarters, 10 pounds of dimes, or 10 pounds of nickels. The choice was hers. She could pick one of the three choices and walk away with the cash.

"That's a lot of coins to worry about," Carlotta worried. "I think the store manager must have been a math teacher once."

"Not as many coins as you might think," Emma said soothingly. "We'll use this postage scale here, the coins that Will's gathering, and a little proportional reasoning."

It took about 10 minutes for the twins to weigh, compute, and tally. Carlotta left their office confident of her choice and happy with the results.

> How should Carlotta take her 10 pounds of winnings? How much money would she win? Explain how you made your decision.

Under Particular Conditions

One day, the twins happened to be watching the TV game show "Find That Dough." "Hey," Emma said, "isn't that Victor?"

Just then the telephone rang. Will answered it.

"Will! you're never going to believe this. It's me, Victor, and I'm calling you from "Find That Dough"—I really am!"

"I know," Will began. "We just saw you—"

"Here's the deal, guys. I have to answer this question to win $1,000. I get one phone call and, you're it."

It was an honor—at least that's what Emma thought. "Fabulous, Victor! How can we help?"

"First off, let's talk faster. I've only got 60 seconds. I have a probability question," he said to Emma and Will and millions of other viewers. "There are 60 books on a shelf—and they all look exactly alike. Twenty are fantasies. Four of the fantasies have 1,000-dollar bills in the binding. I've never even seen a 1,000-dollar bill!"

Neither had the twins. "Your job is to pick one of the books with a bill inside?" asked Emma.

"Not exactly. I have to say what the probability is of choosing a book with money inside *if* I chose a book that was a fantasy in the first place," Victor replied over the air. "If I give the probability correctly, I win."

"Gee, a game show that actually tests your math skills rather than your luck," Emma commented.

"You've got to help me with the math," Victor gulped. "I'm a little nervous in front of all these cameras. Plus, there's a low probability of me answering a probability question correctly anyhow."

"It's not only a probability question, Victor. It's a conditional probability question," Emma informed him. "You've been given information that affects your answer. You already know that you've got a book with money inside."

"I knew I dialed the right number. What should I answer?" Victor was getting pretty excited, but the clock was ticking.

Emma understood conditional probability as well as the next 13-year-old. Normally, she would have just pointed Victor in the right direction. But with so much cash at stake and so little time, Emma gave Victor the correct answer.

"We should try out for shows like this one, Emma," Will told her later.

"Yeah, but what's the probability that one of us would be chosen?" she replied.

What is the probability that a book on the shelf will have money inside it, given that the book is a fantasy?

A Head for Numbers

"Hello, uh, are you the math detective?"

"Will's the name. Math detection's my game," answered Will, who had finished his homework particularly early that day and was in high spirits.

"Well, uh, my name is Alex and I, uh, have a math question."

"Yes, Alex. I'll help if I can. What's up?" said Will, supportively. Alex, he figured, was maybe nine, maybe ten years old, and already pretty good at mumbling.

"Uh, it's not really a math crime or anything. I just need to know something. It's about my big sister, Katie," Alex informed Will.

"OK, Alex, my man. What about your sister? Give me the facts."

Alex told Will that he had been at his desk, had his pencil out, and was about to find the product of 51 and 98, when his sister Katie approached. She had looked over his shoulder and told him the answer was 4,998.

"She's right," noted Will, "but I guess that's not the problem."

"The problem is that she found the answer in about three seconds!" answered a confused Alex. "How did she do it? She won't tell me. She didn't use a calculator or anything."

"She was using number sense. In fact, once we talk about how she did what she did, I'll teach you how to surprise her with a pencil-free-right-off-the-top-of-your-head correct answer to 196 + 97 + 499 + 303! You'll make her head spin like a top!

"What are we waiting for?!" No more "uhs" for Alex. He was ready to show up his show-off big sister.

> How might Will have explained Katie's mental math? How might he have advised Alex to find the sum in his head?

Paying for Peel

"Make no mistake! Granny Smith will not pay for peel!"

Some calls that Emma and Will receive are better suited for consumer-affairs advocates than for 13-year-old math detectives. The call from Granny Smith is an example. Emma answered that one. She instantly put what she had been learning about how to deal with irate clients to work. She was soft-spoken, polite, and soothing.

"Hi. It's Emma here. Tell me more about this peel."

"Oh, you're just a child," Granny squawked. "Here I was, all set to hire you to hustle over to Greg's Grocery and do some of that detective rough stuff like I've seen in the movies. I guess I dialed the wrong kind of detective."

"Wrong for rough-stuff stuff, but right for solving all kinds of number problems. Number problems are job one here, Ms. Smith," Emma said with certainty and a little hard-boiled attitude. "I'm sure we can help."

Apples—
Peels and all
5 pounds for $2.25

"Maybe you can. Maybe you can't. You can start by figuring out how much that thief owes me. Then you can go over there for some rough stuff. You got a big dog or something?"

"No dog. How were you cheated?" Emma asked.

"I bought 7 pounds of apples from that cheap, cheating grocer," Granny said. "He charges $2.25 for 5 pounds of apples. That's high enough, but here's the kicker, kid. Apples have peels. Peels weigh about one-twelfth of the weight of an apple. I'm paying for peel! Peel, I tell you!"

"I didn't know the peel weighed one-twelfth of what the apple weighed," Emma said.

"Well, I know it! I'm not paying for peel!"

"Don't you eat the peel, Ms. Smith?" Emma asked.

"It's Granny, kid. No, I don't eat the peel. I peel it off. That's why it's called a peel. Get it? I peel it off to make pie. You wouldn't want a peel in your pie, would you?"

Emma didn't know what to say. It didn't matter. Before she found something to utter in response, Granny continued with her ranting.

"So what about that rough stuff? Still won't do it? You won't go there with a dog? Big German shepherd or something? Scare some sense into that greedy grocer and get my money back? What about handcuffs? Go in there and slap some cuffs on that crook!"

Emma was clear. "No dog. No cuffs."

"You're in the detective game, and you've got no dog and no cuffs? What kind of detective are you, anyway?"

"The kind that can tell you how much you're paying for peel when you buy apples at Greg's Grocery. That's the kind of detective I am. That's the only kind I am," responded Emma calmly.

"No rough stuff?" Granny asked, much calmer and gentler this time.

"No rough stuff," Emma replied, just as pleasantly.

"OK. All right. So, kid, can you tell me how much I'm paying for apple peels when I buy apples from the fool at that store?"

"Yes ma'am."

"Good for you—and thank you, too. I'll take that information with me next time I buy something from that cheat. In the meantime, I'll bake you one of my best pies," said Granny, almost apologetically. "No peels," she added.

"Thanks. That would be great. I love apple pie. My brother does, too," Emma answered.

"Share the pie with that big dog of yours, too," offered Granny.

> How much does Granny pay for peel when she buys 7 pounds of apples? Explain your solution.

Back in Time

Early one late spring evening—6:15, to be precise—the phone rang in the twins' office. Will answered it.

"Howdy, boy. Jed Tuttle here. Is this Will the detective?"

"Yes, sir, it is," answered Will.

"I am glad as a bumble bee on a hollyhock that you're there to take my call, young fellow! I heard you and your sister are ace math detectives. Have I got a puzzler for you! Are you ready?" Jed asked.

"Ready as a sprinter in starting blocks. Just let me get my sister on the phone so she can hear what you've got to say," said Will.

"Good, yes. Then let's get started, because the 6:30 news starts in fifteen minutes, and I never miss the 6:30 news," Jed added. He told the sleuths his problem, which involved a race against time.

Jed had a brother, Horace, who liked the 6:30 news as much as he did. Horace wasn't there that particular evening. He was on his way to the county fair to show off his sunflowers, the best in the county by far. Horace was going to spend the night at Carlton's house, which was about 35 miles down the road. Horace was traveling very slowly because of his mode of transportation, which was a riding lawn mower. He'd left for Carlton's at 5:00 P.M., traveling at the mower's maximum speed of 8 miles per hour.

"Are you two with me so far?" Jed asked. "Now I'll tell you my problem."

"So far, so good," answered the twins.

 40 Fabulous Math Mysteries Scholastic Professional Books

Jed continued his story. The problem was twofold, he said. In his haste to ride the mower to Carlton's, Horace had taken Jed's wallet instead of his own. Plus, Horace had forgotten his house keys.

"You need to get your wallet back and give your brother his keys and wallet, I bet." said Emma.

"That's it precisely," Jed responded. "There's more, though. I can leave here to go after him at 7:00, when the news ends. I've got to get back by 10:00 tonight because that's when Daisy calls. Daisy is our sister. She calls at 10:00 to talk about the news. We Tuttles keep up with things. Yes we do. We're informed citizens."

"You need to leave at 7:00 and return by 10:00," Will said. "There should be no problem, Mr. Tuttle. Your brother's traveling at 8 miles per hour. You'll surely be able to catch up with him."

"Oh, I'll catch him all right, because I can go after him in the tractor," Jed replied.

"The tractor?" asked Emma.

"Yes, the tractor. Old Reliable, we call it. I can race along in her at, let's see, 20 miles per hour. My question to you is this: If I follow Horace on the county road he took, will I be able to make the wallet switch, remind him of how forgetful he is, and get home in time to discuss today's news with Daisy?"

Will told Jed that he hoped so, but that they would need a minute or two to find out. He took down Jed's phone number and promised to call before the newscast began. That was fine with Jed.

Emma and Will huddled for a minute. They worked together to create a timetable. "Let's make a line graph," Emma said.

"Let's make it a double," Will added.

At 6:25, they were on the phone with Jed Tuttle. By 6:28, Jed had learned that as long as he didn't spend too much time chatting with his brother, and as long as Old Reliable lived up to its name, he would be able to accomplish all that he wanted to accomplish.

"Now that's some good news," said Jed, who was much relieved. He thanked the twins heartily. Then he walked into his den and turned on the TV.

> At what time will Jed and Old Reliable overtake Horace? How far will Horace have driven by then? When will Jed arrive back at his farm? Explain how you arrived at your answers.

Only the Shadow Tells

Emma and Will are nature lovers. They enjoy flowers and trees and warm fragrant breezes on sunny Saturday spring afternoons. One day, when Tabitha called with a question about a tree, Emma jumped at the chance to solve it.

"We were arguing and fighting, which is what my brother Timothy and I normally do on a Saturday. This time our mom had had enough. "If you two can't find something constructive to do, I'll find something for you," Tabitha said, mimicking her mother's annoyed tone. "I certainly could find something constructive to do on my own," she added.

"Timothy couldn't, I suppose," Emma interjected.

"Of course not, so Mom gave us a task," answered Tabitha. "She challenged us to find the height of a large maple tree in our front yard. Can you believe that?"

Emma could see where this was heading. "You can't use a ladder, you can't climb the tree, and you and your brother have no idea where to begin," she guessed.

Tabitha was stunned into silence. That was exactly it.

This was familiar ground to the twins. "Well, you're in luck, Tabitha. It's a beautiful sunny day," Emma said.

"Huh?"

"Do you have a tape measure or yard-stick or anything that you can use to measure a distance along the ground?" she asked the bewildered Tabitha.

40 Fabulous Math Mysteries Scholastic Professional Books

"Uh, yeah, I guess," Tabitha responded.

"Good. Can you rustle up something like a stick or a baseball bat that you can hold upright and measure?" Emma continued.

Tabitha had that, too.

"Then you have the tools you need to figure out the height of the tree."

"I do?" Tabitha asked, somewhat unconvinced.

"Yes, you do," Emma said firmly.

"That's it? That's all the help I'm getting? No other clues? Come on, please."

Emma was a sucker for good begging. It was clue time. "We did discuss what a beautiful and sunny day it was, didn't we?" she pointed out.

"Yes. Beautiful and sunny." Tabitha was still lost. She hoped there was more help coming. There was.

"What do things outside, like trees, have on a sunny day that they don't have on other days?" Emma asked.

"A shadow?"

This girl was no fool. "What about sticks or baseball bats?" Emma asked.

"What about a large maple tree on a front lawn!" Tabitha shouted excitedly. "Especially a large maple tree on a front lawn."

> How can Tabitha and Timothy use the stick and the measuring tape to find the height of the tree?

The Boasters' Club

If you think you've heard everything, then you haven't been to a meeting of the Boasters' Club. Every Tuesday night, the members swap some pretty unbelievable tales. Some tales are taller than others. A sampling of boasts from a recent meeting included the following blasts of bluster:

"I'm such a good swimmer that I swam across the English Channel and back in only two breaths."

"I'm so strong that I can lift 500 pounds with one hand and program the VCR with the other hand."

"I'm so smart that I taught my dog to talk, but I don't think all of his jokes are funny."

"I'm so fast that I can shut off the light by my bedroom door, get across the room, into my bed, and under the covers before the room goes dark."

It was this last boast that caused quite a stir at the Boasters' Club that evening, which is understandable. It was an impossible feat, even for members of the Boasters' Club. It didn't sit well with some of the usual boasters. In an effort to discredit the boast, the whole bunch of boasters called upon the twins. They wanted to prove that the outrageous claim was a downright fib—unlike their own boasts.

One boaster claimed to have run the distance to the twins' office on his hands. Another said she came by ostrich. A third bragged that he balanced a plate of spaghetti on his head while juggling five bowling pins as he walked blindfolded to the office.

They put their story before the twins.

"Under the covers before the room went dark," repeated an amused Will. "That's the boast you're all so bent out of shape about?"

40 Fabulous Math Mysteries Scholastic Professional Books

It was.

"I've done the very same thing myself," Will boasted.

"You have?" answered the ostrich rider.

"Many times. In fact, my sister has done something just as amazing. She dropped an egg 20 feet, and it didn't break," Will claimed. "Twenty feet!" he emphasized.

"I most certainly did," confirmed Emma.

The boasters looked at one another. Smoke was beginning to emerge from their ears. It billowed out when Will explained further and added a few details, such as the fact that he once hopped to bed holding a glass of milk and didn't spill a drop. The boasters thanked the twins for nothing, and left the office squabbling among themselves. Tuesday nights would never be the same again.

How might Will have explained the getting-into-bed boast? How might he have explained the egg-drop feat? List as many possibilities as you can.

A Telling Gift

It was Hector's 16th birthday. Hector is one of old Nat Kudan's nephews. Nat was giving his nephew a birthday gift. It was the nature of the gift that brought Hector to Will and Emma.

"I'll repeat the entire conversation for you," Hector promised. It went something like this:

"I've got a birthday gift here for you, Hector. It's 16 dollars in honor of your 16 years of as a nephew."

"Thanks a bunch, Uncle Nat!"

"I have the 16 dollars right here in my pocket, in 3 bills."

"Three bills, that's great."

"One of them is not a 10-dollar bill, though, and there aren't any coins or partial bills or any tricks like that."

Huh? Hector thought. "How can that be, Uncle Nat?" Hector was a puzzled nephew, which is what he usually was when he dealt with Nat.

After a moment or two of puzzlement, Will and Emma called me. Naturally. They informed me of the conundrum that was before them.

I could have cleared it up for them faster than you could say "pure genius." Instead, I gave them a telling clue. I told them that the answer is in the telling.

It's easy to solve a puzzle when it reminds you of an old gag that you've heard a dozen times before.

> How can you make 16 dollars using exactly and only 3 bills, one of which is not a 10-dollar bill?

Teaching Notes

Meet the Detectives

✳ Although there is no mystery to discuss here, talk with students about what they surmise about the detectives and their mentor from this introduction.

✳ Have students give their ideas about the characteristics of good detectives. Talk with them about some detectives with whom they are familiar. Ask them to identify the precise skills and traits that successful sleuths share.

✳ If none of the students mentions it, point out that good listening skills and good questioning skills are essential for the successful sleuth. Ask them to notice as they read how Will and Emma exhibit these key skills.

✳ As students work through the cases, invite them to write to Will and Emma or to Lump, to offer advice, congratulations, alternate solutions or strategies, or criticisms. Suggest that they present other problems for the twins to tackle.

✳ Point out to students that the 13-year-olds will not capture criminals nor pursue the perpetrators of violent or otherwise serious crimes—those responsibilities are the province of law enforcement agents. Tell them that the "crimes" that face the twin detectives have a decidedly lighter tone. Tell them also that no animals have been harmed in the twins' pursuit of justice.

The CD Collection Crisis

Math Skills/Concepts:

number sense, factors and multiples

Suggested Solution:

Add 1 CD to the gift, for a total of 18 CDs. One-half of 18 is 9; one-third is 6, and one-ninth is 2. Then take back the extra CD. Students can check the solution by adding: 9 + 6 + 2 = 17.

Teaching Tips:

✳ This first problem draws upon students' ability to creatively look at a problem from "outside the lines." Guide them to understand that sometimes they may need to adjust the parameters of a problem in order to solve it.

✳ Provide the hint that although 17 is not divisible by 2, 3, and 6, a number near it is (18).

The Digging Dog Dilemma

Math Skills/Concepts:

measurement: length and area of a circle, properties of circles and squares, visual reasoning

Suggested Solution:

The radius of a circular area of 1,000 sq. ft. is a little less than 18 feet. So 18 feet is the length of the rope. Since the distance from the post to the hedge is 15 feet, Champ's rope reaches less than 3 feet into the neighbor's yard—not far enough for the dog to eat the tulips, even if he stretches a few feet from the end of the rope.

Teaching Tips:

✳ Guide students in making a drawing of the backyards and of the dog and the rope, using the data given. Make sure they see that the rope is a radius of the circular area in which Champ can roam.

✳ As needed, review the meaning of radius and the relationship between it and the area of a circle.

✳ Encourage students to suggest alternate solution strategies; one strategy is simply to stretch out the rope to see how far the end is from the tulips.

The Plucked Pay

whole number operations and operations with percents, order of operations, number sense, mental math

Suggested Solution:

Norman added the four $10 bills to his base pay before calculating his raise and new salary. He shouldn't have; the 25% does not apply to the one-time bonus: $360 x 1.25 + (4 x $10) = $490.

Teaching Tips:

❋ Encourage students to use mental math to solve this one.

❋ You may wish to use this opportunity to discuss finding percents of numbers in real-life situations—calculating increases or decreases in money amounts such as pay raises or cuts, or for finding total prices including sales, taxes, or tips.

A Case of Cast Iron Confusion

Math Skills/Concepts:

Roman numerals, visual reasoning

Suggested Solution:

1874; the markings that show are the top third, approximately, of MDCCCLXXIV.

Teaching Tips:

❋ Discuss that it is common for builders to place the age of the building on a cornerstone and to do so using Roman numerals. Invite interested students to investigate this practice further and to report on their findings.

❋ As needed, point out the clue "gladiator's ghost."

❋ Ask students to look for examples of this kind of dating on commercial buildings in your area. Have them identify other ways that buildings' ages are shown.

The Barbell in the Bag

Math Skills/Concepts:

common multiples

Suggested Solution:

Of the three friends, only Aaron was at the gym on September 29, the day of the theft. All three kids were there together only on every 12th day, beginning with August 2; they were at the gym on August 14 and 26, September 7 and 19, and October 1.

Teaching Tips:

✳ Guide students to make a calendar that includes the days and dates given. They can work forward from August 2, or backward from October 1 to figure out who was at the gym and on what dates.

The Valuable Vase

Math Skills/Concepts:

critical thinking, common sense

Suggested Solution:

The date etched on the vase doesn't make sense; the letters "B.C." would not have been used by people anytime before the time of Christ.

Teaching Tips:

✳ Remind students to read this piece carefully—the fraudulent date may slip past many of them.

✳ Discuss the meaning and use of the letters "B.C." (before Christ) or "B.C.E." (before the common era).

A Case of Too Much Information

Math Skills/Concepts:

measurement (elapsed time), critical thinking, operations with fractions and whole numbers

Suggested Solution:

It will take Eva 18 minutes; she'll be finished at 5:48 P.M. She makes 4 cuts in a board to make 5 pieces; there are 3 boards and, therefore, 12 cuts; 12 x 1.5 = 18. Extra information: length and thickness of each board, the time of Eva's phone call.

Teaching Tips:

✳ Students can assume from the title that there will be unnecessary information given. Admonish them to read the story carefully in order to root out the data that is not needed and focus on what is needed to solve the problem.

✳ Discuss why certain data is unnecessary for the solution of the problem. For example, ask a student to explain why knowing the length and width of each board is not useful information (her sawing speed is given).

✳ Invite a student to explain why it takes 4 cuts to make 5 pieces. Check understanding by asking how many cuts are needed for 8 pieces and for 408 pieces.

A Case of Too Little Information

Math Skills/Concepts:

critical thinking, algebraic representation and modeling

Suggested Solution:
He needs to know how many grandchildren Ralph has.

Teaching Tips:

✳ Discuss why this problem cannot be solved as presented.

✳ You may want to invite students to suggest a number of grandchildren and then solve the resulting problem. For instance, if Ralph had 4 grandchildren, the problem could be solved by writing and solving the following equation: let x = the amount the youngest grandchild gets:
$x + (x + 5) + (x + 10) + (x + 15) = 100$

✳ Students can also guess, and then adjust their guess to solve the problem.

Mixed-Up Identities

Math Skills/Concepts:

organizing data, making inferences, logical reasoning

Suggested Solution:

Clark lives in South Dakota, has blue eyes, and drives a truck.
Milton lives in Texas, has brown eyes, and drives a sport utility vehicle (SUV).
Terry lives in California, has green eyes, and drives a motorcycle.
Sal lives in Maine, has brown eyes, and drives a convertible.

Teaching Tips:

✳ This is the first of four mysteries that can be solved most easily by recording data in a table and then using that organized data to make logical inferences. The other stories are MIXED-UP WINNERS, IN A PICKLE, and MASCOT MISCHIEF.

✳ Talk about what information is given in the problem, and what information students need to find out. Have them identify what the categories of information are (name, state, kind of vehicle, color of eyes). Discuss the advantages of recording the data in an organized fashion. Ask students to present ways to do this.

✳ Suggest that one way is for students to make and fill in a 4 x 4 table. You may want to have them work in pairs to do this. Have partners explain to each other the inferences they make from the data given.

✳ You may find it useful to invite a volunteer to put his or her table on the overhead projector or board and explain how he or she used known information recorded in the table to fill in the rest of the table.

Squabbling Siblings

Math Skills/Concepts:

number sense

Suggested Solution:

A book would not have 117 and 118 as facing pages; on facing pages, the page on the left is always an even numbered page and the one on the right, an odd numbered page.

Teaching Tips:

✳ The even-odd problem here may escape students at first. Guide them to open any book before giving up on finding the solution.

A Cool Witness

Math Skills/Concepts:

rational numbers, measurement (temperature)

Suggested Solution:

It was not a cold day. 15°C is equivalent to about 59°F, which is a mild temperature by most standards. The witness would not have been freezing, and the thief would not have been wearing a down coat.

Teaching Tips:

✳ You may want to briefly discuss the roles (defense and prosecution) of the different attorneys, and of other participants in a courtroom during a trial like this one. Explain any courtroom procedures or court-related language used in this story, as needed.

✳ Also, as needed, review the distinction between Celsius and Fahrenheit temperature scales. Discuss a formula to use (here's one: °F = $\frac{9}{5}$ x °C + 32) to convert a temperature given in one scale to the equivalent temperature in the other. You may wish to use this opportunity to review other relationships between Celsius and Fahrenheit scales. You may also find it useful to discuss benchmark temperatures students can easily use to compare temperatures in the two scales.

Irritating Inheritance

Math Skills/Concepts:

algebraic representation and modeling, fractions

Suggested Solution:

Libby—$12,000; Hector—$30,000; Dave—$60,000

Teaching Tips:

✳ Make sure students understand the relationships between the sizes of the three inheritances. Then guide them to represent each of the inheritances using an algebraic expression, and then to write and solve an equation to solve the problem. One possible equation to use is $x + \frac{5}{2}x + 5x = 102,000$, where x represents the smallest inheritance, the amount of money Libby will receive. Invite students to suggest other equations to use.

✳ Some students may guess and then adjust their guesses to solve the problem. Ask them to explain their reasoning. One way: First determine which of the nephews or nieces gets the smallest part of the inheritance; choose a reasonable money amount for that niece or nephew; use that amount to find the others; adjust it as needed to fit the requirements of the problem.

A Ticklish Tip Problem

Math Skills/Concepts:

number sense, fractions

Suggested Solution:

Each server should get $18 in tips. There was a total of $54 in tips to start.

Teaching Tips:

✳ Review with students the information that is given in the problem and what they can infer from it. For instance, begin by eliciting from them how much money was in the jar when Danielle reached in ($24, since she left $16 after taking her third—$8). Make sure students understand that each of the other servers took $\frac{1}{3}$ and left $\frac{2}{3}$ of what was in the jar when she or he reached in.

✳ Guide students to work backwards to determine how much money was in the jar before each of the other two servers reached in. For instance, they can go next to Felix, who was the second one to take his tips. Students can know that he left $24. Ask, "How much money did Felix take if he took a third, which left $24 in the jar? ($12) How much was in the jar when he reached in for his share?" ($36) Students can use these answers to determine how much Ellie took and left. With those final pieces of information, they can figure out how much money was in the jar to begin with.

✳ Have students explain how they reached their solutions. Invite them to suggest ways for the servers at Carla's to avoid this problem in the future.

The Bad Art Burglary

Math Skills/Concepts:

proportional reasoning, measurement (time), prime numbers, palindromes

Suggested Solution:

The robbery took place at 7:45 A.M. The license plate number is 64946.

Teaching Tips:

✳ There are two problems for students to solve in this story. Make sure they understand the information presented. Guide students to first figure out the time of the robbery and then to determine the license plate number.

✳ You may want to have students work in pairs.

✳ Students may have success by guessing robbery times and then checking and adjusting those guesses. Visual learners may benefit by looking at an analog clock. Ask students to explain the method they used to figure out the time.

✳ Review the meaning of palindromes and of prime numbers, as needed. Some students may benefit by making a list of prime numbers less than 30. Invite volunteers to explain how they used all the clues to figure out the remaining numbers of the license plate. Ask them to explain the usefulness of Nat's final clue.

Mixed-Up Winners

Math Skills/Concepts:

organizing data, making inferences, logical reasoning

Suggested Solution:

Maria—math, Edgar—science, Kim—creative writing, Tom—art

Teaching Tips:

✳ This problem is similar in nature to MIXED-UP IDENTITIES. Talk about what information is given in the problem, and what information students need to find out. Have them identify what the categories of information are. Guide students to record in an organized way all the data Jack provides. Talk about ways to do this.

✳ You may want to have students work in pairs. Have partners discuss the inferences they make from the data given.

✳ You may find it useful to invite a volunteer to put his or her table on the overhead projector or board, and then explain how he or she used known information recorded in the table to fill in the rest of the table.

Celebrity (pause) Seating

Math Skills/Concepts:

number sense, whole number operations, pattern recognition

Suggested Solution:

The hall has 735 seats.

Teaching Tips:

✳ The solution to this problem involves finding sums of consecutive numbers. The most efficient way to do that is to recognize and use a pattern. To begin, you may want to start with a simpler problem, as an example. For instance, have students find the sums of the numbers from 1 to 10. Work through this simpler problem together. Guide students to recognize that it can be solved by finding five sums of 11: 1 + 10, 2 + 9, 3 + 8, and so on.

✳ Encourage students to use that same strategy to find the number of seats in the hall. Ask them to tell what information they will need in order to do so (the number of seats in the 30th row). Discuss how they can use a pattern to find that number (one way: List the number of seats in the first few rows to notice that each row has 9 more seats than the number of the row; using that pattern, they can see that row number 30 will have 39 seats). Reminding students of the simpler problem above, ask, "What is the sum of seats in rows 1 and 30?" (49) "In rows 2 and 29?" (49) Then ask, "How many pairs of rows with sums of 49 are there?" (15) Lastly, ask, "How can you use this information to find the total number of seats in rows 1 through 30?" (Multiply 49 by 15.)

✳ Recognize and support other expressions of this pattern or other patterns students find and use to solve this problem. Extend by challenging students to use a pattern to find the sums of the numbers 1-100 or 1-1,000.

In a Pickle

Math Skills/Concepts:

organizing data, making inferences, logical reasoning

Suggested Solution:

toaster—Ankers, blender—Reids, candlesticks—Wixteds, salad bowl—Motts

Teaching Tips:

✳ This problem is similar in nature to MIXED-UP IDENTITIES and MIXED-UP WINNERS. Once again, have students begin by identifying what information is given in the problem and what information they need to find out. Guide them again to record in an organized way all the data the Picketts provide. Discuss ways to do this.

❋ You may want to have students work in pairs. Have partners discuss the inferences they make from the data they've recorded.

❋ Ask a volunteer to put his or her table on the overhead projector or board. Ask the volunteer to explain how he or she used what the table shows to fill in the missing data. Invite discussion.

A Case from Space

Math Skills/Concepts:

ratios, critical (and imaginative!) thinking

Suggested Solution:

Yes; on Mercury, Kenneth would be 20 years old.

Teaching Tips:

❋ This mystery requires students to suspend their sense of disbelief long enough to tackle a problem filled more with fantasy and fun than with middle-school mathematics. If needed, point out to students that there are (as of this writing) no signs of life on the planet Mercury, and that even if there were, the likelihood that life would have a close physical resemblance to that on Earth would be minimal, at best. Students shouldn't have too much trouble accepting the idea that "Mercurians" can drive a car and even have automotive preferences!

❋ Tell students that using real data about the solar system can help them solve the perplexing mystery in this story. They can use an almanac or other source to see that Mercury, which is closer to the sun than the earth is, has an orbit of about 88 days—about one-fourth of the time it takes the earth to make one revolution. By deduction, 1 year on Earth is equal to about 4 years on Mercury. That 1:4 ratio explains how Kenneth "aged" 8 years in the two years he was away.

Grappling over Grades

Math Skills/Concepts:

statistical measures of average

Suggested Solution:

The mode of Lucia's test scores is 91; the mean of the scores is about 73.14. The mean is the more reasonable representation of her performance on the tests.

Teaching Tips:

* This debate over the interpretation of test scores is a good starting point for a discussion about the different measures of center and spread, and the usefulness of each measure in analyzing given situations. Talk, for instance, about real-life situations for which the mode is a more appropriate measure than the mean, or for when it is the median that is the most useful measure of average. Discuss times when knowing the range of data is very important.

* Discuss why, in Lucia's case, the mean more accurately describes her test results than the mode does. Ask students to give the median of her scores (66), and to explain why that is or is not a useful measure of her test performances.

* Challenge students to list two sets of seven test scores for Lucia, one for which the mode is the most accurate description of the data, and one for which the median works best. Discuss their choices.

Case of Appearances

Math Skills/Concepts:

correspondence between data sets and graphical representation of the data

Suggested Solution:

Although the graphs show the same information, they differ in appearance due to differences in the horizontal and vertical scales and to differences in increments shown on the vertical scales. Augie's graph shows a more gradual increase in prices for two reasons; (1) there is more space between the years along the horizontal axis, and (2) there are greater increments along the vertical scale.

Teaching Tips:

* Help students interpret these graphs, as needed. Have them describe the

information given along the axes. Guide them to notice that both graphs show the same data and that both have compressed vertical scales. Ask students if they think the graphs are correctly titled. Talk about the idea that by changing the scales of a line graph (or a bar graph), you can change the impression the graph creates about a set of data. Discuss that graphs can be misleading, too.

✳ Challenge students to think of other ways for the K.A.R.P. kids to make their graph show a rapid rise in prices, and for Augie to make his show a gradual increase. Have students make their new graphs and then explain how the graphs create the impression they were intended to create.

✳ Have students make bar graphs or pictographs that show the same data the line graphs do. Challenge them to construct their graphs to show either Augie's or the kids' point of view. Ask them to explain the choices they made in a brief expository essay.

✳ Encourage students to look in newspapers, magazines, and online for real-life examples of graphs, plots, or tables that advertisers make and graphs, plots, or tables that consumer groups make. Have the class discuss the components of these displays and to identify ways that they do or do not make the case they were intended to make.

The Weight of the Fake Figurine

Math Skills/Concepts:
measurement, critical thinking, logical reasoning

Suggested Solution:
(1) Weigh any six of the figurines, three on a pan. (2) If the pans balance, the fake is not among the figurines weighed—weigh the remaining two figurines; the lighter one is the fake. (3) If the pans don't balance, the pan that weighs less has the fake—weigh any two of the three figurines from that pan; if they balance, the remaining one is the fake; if they don't, the lighter one of the two weighed is the fake.

Teaching Tips:
✳ Encourage students to try different methods and to discuss their findings. If you have a balance scale, make it available; it may be of benefit to tactile learners. Then invite a student to explain why the solution strategy presented above works.

* Present a similar problem, but one in which the fake weighs more than the genuine object does. Ask students to explain how they would adjust their strategies to find the fake then.

Mascot Mischief

Math Skills/Concepts:

organizing data, making inferences, logical reasoning

Suggested Solution:

Marcy took it; she had the key to the biology lab.

Teaching Tips:

* This problem is similar in nature to MIXED-UP IDENTITIES, MIXED-UP WINNERS, and IN A PICKLE. Here, students need to identify information given in the problem, and then to use it to rule out four suspects in order to find the one responsible for a theft. Guide them again to record in an organized fashion all the data the pranksters' note provides. Discuss ways to do this. Note: The key piece of information that the log lived in the biology lab is not presented until all the other information is given. Students need to read the entire story before making and using their tables.

* You may want to let students work in pairs. Have partners discuss the inferences they make from the data they've recorded.

* Invite a volunteer to put his or her table on the overhead projector or board. Ask the volunteer to explain how he or she used what the table shows to fill in the missing data.

The Sweet Tooth Robberies

Math Skills/Concepts:

number patterns, measurement (elapsed time)

Suggested Solution:

The thief will strike again on March 4, if he/she sticks to his/her established pattern (unless it's a leap year).

Teaching Tips:

✳ Guide students to look for a pattern in the dates of the robberies. Some may express the pattern as $2x + 1$. Others may describe it like this (or in words that mean the same thing): The difference in days between each pair of robbery dates is twice as great as the difference in days between the preceding pair of robbery dates.

✳ Students will need to consult a calendar to find the date of the thief's next strike.

✳ Challenge students to find the date of the strike after the one on March 4. (May 7)

Fair Fares?

Math Skills/Concepts:

proportional reasoning, operations with money amounts

Suggested Solution:

Maureen's proportional reasoning was faulty; the part of each ride for which Red charges $2.50 constitutes a greater or lesser fraction of that ride depending on the distance of the ride. For the shorter ride Maureen took, the first fifth of a mile (at $2.50), was a greater fraction of the whole length of the ride than it was in the second trip she took.

Teaching Tips:

✳ Discuss the value of using proportional reasoning to solve many different kinds of problems. Elicit from students several real-life applications of this kind of reasoning.

✳ Guide students to see where Maureen made her error. Ask them to role-play how Emma might explain Maureen's error to her.

✳ Have a student show and explain how to determine the price of any cab ride with Red, and of the two rides from the story, in particular.

✳ Extend by having students find out what taxi drivers charge in your area. Have them use those real rates to figure out the cost of different trips. You may want to provide local street maps for that purpose.

A View from Above

Math Skills/Concepts:

visual (and creative) reasoning

Suggested Solutions:

1) Two skiers, each on one ski, ski down the slope, around the tree, one to the left, one to the right. 2) One skier, on one ski, skies twice down the slope, once going to the left of the tree, once to the right. 3) One very tall skier skies right over the very short tree. 4) One tall, strong skier skies right over the small, bendable tree, bending it forward as he/she passes. 5) One skier skies down the slope, stops right at the tree; a second skier drops down from the tree, or is waiting just on the other side of the tree, and continues down the slope, using and continuing the tracks made by the first skier. 6) One skier went to the left of the tree, another to the right of the tree; one ski track was erased on each side. 7) One skier comes up the slope to meet the tracks of a skier who comes down the slope. One skier skies down the hill to the tree, climbs the tree, comes down on the other side, then finds and continues the tracks.

Teaching Tips

✳ Other explanations are possible. Encourage students to be imaginative. Invite them to share their ideas. Keep a running list. See who can come up with the most creative ideas. Invite interested students to sketch some of their ideas, as needed, to clarify the ideas for themselves or classmates.

✳ You may extend the problem by changing it. For instance, have the rangers spot footprints rather than ski tracks going around the tree—right-foot-only tracks to the right of the tree, left-foot-only tracks to the left of the tree.

Playing a Crook's Game

Math Skills/Concepts:

spatial reasoning and shape recognition, logical thinking

Suggested Solution:

Coded message—The loot is in the basement of the old brewery on Miller Road.

Teaching Tips

✳ Demonstrate on the board or on an overhead projector how to use the tic-tac-toe form of code. Discuss and show how each letter is represented by a unique cell shape. You may wish to have students practice the code by deciphering a word or two, or even a brief message. Then ask a volunteer to show how to decode the crook's message.

✳ Challenge small groups of students to practice using this kind of code to create and decode messages of their own. Invite them to use the tic-tac-toe code format to respond to the thief.

✳ Have students introduce, talk about, and demonstrate other types of codes they know.

A Brief Reply

Math Skills/Concepts:

logical thinking, number sense

Suggested Solution:

Coded message—You were lucky this time.

Teaching Tips:

✳ Students will soon recognize the difficulty inherent in deciphering messages that use the telephone number pad code—there are three or more letters for each number (some number pads have the letters Q and Z). Therefore, it will be useful to discuss other clues that can help kids decode messages, such as (1) noticing the number of letters a word has, (2) recognizing digits that repeat in a message, (3) knowing which letters appear most often in words, and (4) understanding where certain letters are often found or not found in words. To give an example of this last form of clue, point out to students that if the number 8 appears at the end of a word, it is much more likely to represent a *t* than either a *u* or a *v*.

✳ Students will have an easier time deciphering this coded message if they have a telephone number pad to look at. You may wish to have a student copy one from a telephone onto the board or onto an overhead projector screen.

✳ Invite students to make their own reply to the sleuths, or to the crook, using this code.

Just Her Luck

Math Skills/Concepts:

permutations and the fundamental counting principle, measurement (time)

Suggested Solution:

If Kisha could not find the right combination until the very last one she tried, she would have spent nearly $6\frac{3}{4}$ hours trying. If so, she could not have finished in time to commit the bank burglary, which took place at 6 P.M.

Teaching Tips:

✳ Review all the information that students know—(1) the time Kisha began to try the combinations, (2) the numbers on the safe's combination lock, and (3) the arrangement of them that will open it, (4) the time it takes her to try every arrangement of three numbers, and (5) the time the bank was robbed.

✳ Discuss what *permutations* are (an ordered arrangement of numbers), and why finding the correct 3-number set of numbers that will open the safe's lock is an example of using the concept of permutations.

✳ Discuss the fundamental counting property, and then ask a student to demonstrate how to use it to quickly find the number of permutations possible given the numbers on the safe's lock (24 x 23 x 22 = 12,144). Discuss the meaning of the term *factorial*, and show how to use its symbol (!).

✳ Then talk about how to use the idea of permutation, along with the information given in the problem, to determine that Kisha could not have finished in time to also rob the bank (at 2 seconds per permutation, a total of 24,288 seconds, or 6.747 hours; 6.746 hours past 11:30 A.M. is about 6:15 P.M., too late for the bank job).

A Timely Call

Math Skills/Concepts:

measurement (time and time zones)

Suggested Solution:

At 7 P.M. in California, it is 10 P.M. in Eastern Standard time, where Boston is. At that time, it is dark outside; there would've been no sun in the caller's eyes.

Teaching Tips

✳ As needed, review the locations of the different time zones on the map of the continental United States. You may wish to have students examine a map showing the time zones and identify the time zone location for several large cities or places of interest.

✳ Ask a variety of questions to test students' understanding of time zones and how they are part of our lives. Ask, for instance, what time a TV program is on the air in San Diego, CA, Miami, FL, and Denver, CO, when it airs in Dallas, TX at 1 P.M. (11 A.M., 2 P.M., and noon, respectively) Talk about the importance of using time zone information for advertisers, politicians, TV network executives, and newspaper publishers, among others.

Pigs in a Pen

Math Skills/Concepts:

number sense, critical (and creative) thinking

Suggested Solution:

There could be 9 pigs in each of three pens; all three pens are within one larger pen.

| 9 | 9 | 9 |

Teaching Tips:

✳ This is an Aha! kind of problem that is best solved by examining assumptions. Once students understand that there's more (or less) than meets the eye here, they could have an easier time finding a solution that meets the requirements.

✳ Guide stumped students to work with sketches or with counters and string. Encourage all students to discuss their approaches and to explain their answers. They should know that the sum of 4 odd numbers is an even number.

Row, Row, Row Your Boat

Math Skills/Concepts:

number sense, logical reasoning

Suggested Solution:

The kids, May and June, row across to the mainland. One rows back to the island.

Ed, the father, rows across alone. The other child returns to the island. Both kids row across to the mainland again. One rows back to the island. April, the mother, crosses to the mainland alone. The other child rows back to the island. Both kids row to the mainland once again. Now all Balins are off the island.

Teaching Tips:

❋ Begin by reviewing the information that the Balin family knows—they know their weights and they know how much weight their small boat can hold. Discuss that in addition to knowing what the Balins can't do, students also know what the family can do—the children can fit in the boat at the same time.

❋ That tip alone may not be enough to help kids solve the problem. As they had to in the previous mystery, kids may need to change their assumptions to come up with a workable solution. They may need a nudge to help them realize that there is something else the Balins can do—they can have family members return to the island if necessary. Nothing in the problem limits return trips. Decide whether your students need this additional hint.

Flavors of the Day

Math Skills/Concepts:

combinations

Suggested Solution:

Gilbert can serve 28 two-scoop combinations.

Teaching Tips:

❋ This problem calls upon students' understanding of the concept of combinations. As needed, discuss that a combination is a set of items in which order is not important. In the case of the ice cream parlor servings, the items are the ice cream scoops. The order in which they appear in the cones or cups does not matter; in a vanilla-chocolate cup or cone, the chocolate can be either on top or on the bottom. In general, the symbol $_nC_r$ denotes the number of combinations of r items chosen from a set of n items. A formula for $_nC_r$ is $_nP_r \div r!$, where P represents the number of permutations.

❋ According to information in the problem, Cones ordinarily serves 66 two-scoop combinations. To do so, they need to have 12 different flavors on hand.

Students can work backwards to figure this out. Here's how: They can use the symbol $_nC_r$ to represent the combination of some number of flavors of ice cream taken 2 at a time. They can infer that some number divided by 2!, or 2, yields 66. That number is 132. Then they can deduce that 12 x 11 gives 132 permutations. They can use the symbol $_{12}C_2$ to represent the combination of 12 flavors of ice cream taken 2 at a time.

✳ Now students can solve the problem. If 4 flavors weren't available for Gilbert to serve that day, then the store only had 8 flavors on hand. The symbol $_8C_2$ represents the combination of 8 flavors of ice cream taken 2 at a time; (8 x 7) ÷ 2! = 28.

Carlotta's Coins

Math Skills/Concepts:

number sense (money amounts), proportional reasoning, measurement (weight)

Suggested Solution:

Carlotta should take the quarters; she wins about $200 by doing so.

Teaching Tips:

✳ Provide a scale, like a postal scale; students will need to weigh coins to solve the problem. Encourage them to first guess which coins will be worth the most and the least. You may wish to have students work with partners.

✳ Since it is unlikely that students will have 10 pounds of any of these coins handy, guide them to measure lesser weights, and then use proportional reasoning to find out how many of each coin are needed to make a weight of 10 pounds.

✳ Have students describe their weighing strategies and why they chose them. (One reasonable approach to selecting a weight is to use a factor of 16— there are 16 ounces in a pound; students might find the number of coins that weigh 4 ounces, or even 2 ounces or 1 ounce.)

✳ Students' weighings and calculations should show that a pound of quarters has about 80 quarters, that a pound of dimes has about 192 dimes, and that a pound of nickels has about 88 nickels. So, 10 pounds of quarters is worth about $200, 10 pounds of dimes is worth $192, and 10 pounds of nickels is worth $44.

Under Particular Conditions

Math Skills/Concepts:

probability and conditional probability

Suggested Solution:

The probability is $\frac{1}{5}$.

Teaching Tips:

❋ As needed, review with students how to find the probability of an event occurring. Discuss that a problem such as this one involves conditional probability, since a particular condition has reduced the size of the sample space. In this case, the sample space has been reduced by the fact that Victor already knows that the book he has selected is a fantasy.

❋ Guide students to see that if their task were simply to find the probability of choosing a book with money inside, they would multiply the probability of choosing a fantasy ($\frac{20}{60}$, or $\frac{1}{3}$), by the probability of choosing a fantasy with a bill inside ($\frac{1}{5}$). Then elicit that since Victor already knows he has selected a fantasy, to find the probability that the book has money inside, he needs to divide by the probability of choosing a fantasy: $(\frac{1}{3} \times \frac{1}{5}) \div \frac{1}{3} = \frac{1}{5}$.

❋ You may want to discuss with students the kinds of conditions that will reduce a sample space. Ask them to explain what happens to the probability of an event occurring when the sample space is reduced in size. (It increases.)

A Head for Numbers

Math Skills/Concepts:

whole-number operations, mental math, distributive property

Suggested Solution:

Katie may have multiplied 51 x 100, then subtracted 102, which is the product of 2 x 51. The advice to Alex might be to add the compatible numbers 97 + 303 for a sum of 400, add the rounded numbers 200 + 500 (196 + 499) for a sum of 700 to that, and then subtract 5, for a total of 1,095.

Teaching Tips:

❋ As needed, review the distributive property as a tool students can use to multiply mentally. Ask a student to show and explain how Katie used the distributive property to find the product so quickly.

❋ Discuss with students that there are many strategies they can use to find sums or products mentally. You may wish to use this opportunity to review some of these together. Students may benefit from a discussion of the many everyday real-life uses for mental math skills.

❋ Invite students to suggest other ways for Katie to have done her mental math. Then have them demonstrate other strategies Alex could be shown to find his sums mentally.

Paying for Peel

Math Skills/Concepts:

operations with fractions and money amounts, proportional reasoning, measurement

Suggested Solution:

Granny pays about $0.26 for peel when she buys 7 pounds of apples.

Teaching Tips:

❋ Guide students to see that the solution to this mystery involves solving a multi-step problem involving fractions and money amounts. Ask a volunteer to explain how to use proportional reasoning, and the grocer's 5-pound rate for apples, to figure out the price of 7 pounds of apples.

❋ You may wish to invite a student to demonstrate how to use the distributive property to find the price for 7 pounds of apples using mental math (one way: $3\frac{1}{2}$ x $0.90 = (3 x $0.90) + ($\frac{1}{2}$ x $0.90) = 0.315).

❋ Extend by inviting students to figure out how much extra they pay for peels (or pits, seeds, skins, or cobs) when they buy other fruits and vegetables. You may prefer to assign this messy task for homework.

Back in Time

Math Skills/Concepts:

double-line graphs, distance formula

Suggested Solution:

Jed will overtake Horace at about 8:20 P.M. and will be back at his farm at about 9:40 P.M.

Teaching Tips:

✳ As needed, review and discuss the formula for finding distance: $d = rt$, and how to use the formula to find rate of speed and time traveled.

✳ Have grid paper and rulers available for students.

✳ Guide students to begin by making a table that shows the distances both Horace and Jed travel, for several hours, given their rates of speed. Then encourage them to show this information on a double line graph, where one line represents Horace in his mower, and the other, Jed in his tractor. As needed, discuss how to construct a double-line graph, including which data, and in what increments, to place on the axes of the graph. Remind students to label the features of their graphs and to give them a title.

✳ Once students have constructed their graphs, ask them to explain how these show the time when Jed will overtake Horace (where the graphs intersect). Ask them to explain the difference in the slopes of the two lines. (The graph of Jed's trip is steeper; he's traveling $2\frac{1}{2}$ times as fast as Horace.)

Only the Shadow Tells

Math Skills/Concepts:

proportional reasoning, indirect measurement

Suggested Solution:

Tabitha and Timothy can stand a stick (or pencil or bat) in the ground. They measure its height and its shadow. They measure the shadow of the tree. To find the height of the tree, they can write and solve a proportion.

Teaching Tips

✳ The concept at the heart of the solution to this problem is that in a particular place and at a given time of day, the ratio of the height of an object and the length of the shadow it casts will be the same for any object and its shadow. In other words, if a 10-ft. pole casts a 5-ft. shadow, then a 6-ft. tall person standing next to it will cast a 3-ft. shadow.

✳ Ask a student to write a proportion Tabitha and Timothy might use to solve their problem. (possible answer: stick height/stick shadow = tree height/tree shadow)

✳ You may wish to have pairs of students, armed with tape measure and pencil and paper, try this strategy to figure out the height of a tall object nearby, such as a tree, a flagpole, or even a golden arch.

The Boasters' Club

Math Skills/Concepts:

common sense, non-routine problems

Suggested Solution:

It was not dark when the person got into bed because it was daytime. Emma could drop an egg 20 feet without breaking it under the following conditions (among others):

—if she dropped it into a liquid or onto a very soft surface
—if it was caught by somebody after it had dropped 20 feet
—if it broke after it had dropped more than 20 feet
—if it was hard-boiled

Teaching Tips:

✳ These are the kinds of problems in which students' ability to adjust their assumptions will serve them well. When you are talking about solutions to these boasts, discuss how what students have come to understand compares with what they originally assumed.

✳ Encourage students to come up with as many possible solutions as they can for both boasts. Have them share and explain their ideas. Encourage creative thinking!

✳ Invite students to challenge classmates with any problems of this nature that they know.

A Telling Gift

Math Skills/Concepts:

number sense, non-routine problems

Suggested Solution:

One of the bills is not a 10-dollar bill, the other one is. Nat has one 10-dollar bill, one 5-dollar bill, and one 1-dollar bill.

Teaching Tips:

✳ This is another non-routine problem. Guide puzzled students to listen very carefully to the question asked. If there are still no light bulbs going on, try reading the question again. But this time, read it with emphasis that makes the solution more apparent. Then duck.

✳ You may wish to annoy students with the following brain stretcher:

Place a dime and a quarter together on a table so that there is no space between them. Then place a nickel between the dime and the quarter without moving the quarter or touching the dime. (One answer: Place a finger on the quarter to hold it in place. With your other hand, place the nickel on the desk on the side of the quarter opposite from where the dime is. Put a finger on the nickel so you can move it along the desk. Then hit the quarter with the nickel, hard enough to force the dime away from it. Place the nickel in the open space between the dime and the quarter. Have a student demonstrate this for the others.)

✳ Invite students to share non-routine problems they know.

Name _____ Date _____

?　8　?　?　?　A　?　9　?　6　?　3　?　1　?　5　?　1

Investigator's Log

Name of case _____

Restate the problem in your own words: _____

_____

_____

_____

_____

What information do you have? _____

_____

_____

_____

_____

What information do you need? _____

_____

_____

_____

_____

What can you do to solve the problem? _____

_____

_____

_____

_____

Solution: _____

_____

_____

_____

How do you know your solution makes sense? _____

_____

_____

_____

_____

Certificate of Recognition

for

Excellence

as a

Math Sleuth

is hereby
presented to

_____

Congratulations!

_____

(teacher's name)